THE CONSTITUTIVE ELEMENTS OF PARISHES
A HISTORICAL SYNOPSIS AND A COMMENTARY

The Catholic University of America
Canon Law Studies
No. 296

The Constitutive Elements of Parishes

A Historical Synopsis and a Commentary

BY THE

REV. ANTHONY BERNARD MICKELLS, J.C.L.

Priest of the Archdiocese of Omaha

A DISSERTATION

SUBMITTED TO THE FACULTY OF THE SCHOOL OF CANON LAW OF THE CATHOLIC UNIVERSITY OF AMERICA IN PARTIAL FULFILLMENT OF THE REQUIREMENTS FOR THE DEGREE OF DOCTOR OF CANON LAW

The Catholic University of America Press
Washington, D. C.
1950

NIHIL OBSTAT:

JOANNES ROGG SCHMIDT, J.C.D.
Censor Deputatus

Washingtonii, die 7 augusti 1950

IMPRIMATUR:

✠ GERALDUS T. BERGAN, D.D.
Archiepiscopus Omahensis

Omahae, die 14 augusti 1950

MURRAY & HEISTER
WASHINGTON, D. C.

PRINTED BY
TIMES AND NEWS PUBLISHING CO.
GETTYSBURG, PA., U. S. A.

TABLE OF CONTENTS

TABLE OF CONTENTS (Continued)

TABLE OF CONTENTS (Continued)

FOREWORD

The life of the parish is the life of the Church. As the parish prospers, so prospers the Church. These axioms certainly call for no proof. The parish is recognized as the vital unit in ecclesiastical organization, just as the family is recognized as the nuclear unit in civil organization. It is not surprising, then, that much has been written regarding the parish. Only a few other canonical institutes have merited the replete historical treatment accorded it. Yet, though one can find some incidental consideration given to the various elements constitutive of parishes, one would search in vain for a distinct study of that question in a composite form.

It is the purpose of this dissertation to fill that lacuna in at least some manner, imperfect though it may be.

The reader will note that in both the historical synopsis and the canonical commentary of this study an effort has been made to accord a distinct and separate treatment to each of the constitutive elements of parishes. One could object to this manner of presentation by declaring that the historical development of the respective elements was of a concurrent character, and that even now one can hardly comment upon one element to the exclusion of the others. While this is partially true, the writer nevertheless felt that there was sufficient justification for his mode of presentation.

As is explained later in the body of this study, the granting of a separate historical treatment to each element is warranted by the fact that the history of the parochial institute is very vague. Seemingly the only possible manner in which to present the matter in clear fashion was through the method herein employed. A discussion of the several elements under distinct chapters in the canonical commentary is similarly justified. A commentary on the elements as a whole would lead only to confusion. Admittedly there are distinct disadvantages in the adopted mode of procedure. Repetition is inevitable, and it becomes difficult to present a composite picture of the parochial institute as it is. Nevertheless these hindrances are outweighed by the consideration of clarity with which the respective constituents may be identified and thus presented to the reader.

Although some effort was made to divide the dissertation into two parts, a historical synopsis and a canonical commentary, it will be noted that historical notes are not entirely excluded from the canonical commentary. The reason for this method is evident. At times it is not possible to understand the present law except in the light of its historical background. Hence, at the expense of being repetitious, the writer did not neglect in the second part of his study to include notes which had already been presented in the historical synopsis.

The writer wishes to express his sincere gratitude to His Excellency, the Most Reverend Gerald T. Bergan, D.D. and his grateful remembrance of the late Most Reverend James H. Ryan, S.T.D., Archbishops of Omaha, for the opportunity to pursue graduate study in Canon Law. He also wishes to express his thanks to the members of the Faculty of the School of Canon Law for their help and direction in the preparation of this work, to his fellow students for their aid, and to his family and friends for their encouragement.

PART I

Preliminary Notions and Historical Synopsis

CHAPTER I

PRELIMINARY NOTIONS

The specific purpose of this study is to present a historical synopsis and a canonical commentary on the constitutive elements of parishes. Before such a project is attempted, however, it is decidedly advisable to establish some general preliminary notions.

ARTICLE 1. DEFINITION OF TERMS

A. *Parish*

In the first place, what is meant by the term "parish?" Commentators have defined it in various ways. It can mean a territory, circumscribed by well defined limits, in which dwell the faithful who *ex officio* are committed to the care of a proper pastor;[1] or a church to which is assigned a specific group of the faithful who live in a certain territory and are placed under the care of a proper pastor;[2] or thirdly, a determinate group of the faithful who are assigned to a particular church and over whom presides *ex officio* a rector as their proper pastor for the care of their souls.[3]

In a search for a concise definition of the generic term "parish," however, the first two definitions must be rejected as too narrow,

---

[1] Pirhing, *Jus Canonicum in Quinque Libros Decretalium Distributum* (5 vols. in 4, Dilingae, 1674-1678), Lib. III, tit. 29, n. 1 (hereafter cited Pirhing); Reiffenstuel, *Ius Canonicum Universum* (5 vols. in 7, Venetiis, 1735), Lib. III, tit. 29, n. 3 (hereafter cited Reiffenstuel); Rossi, *De Paroecia* (Romae: Pustet, 1923), p. 60; Coronata, *Institutiones Iuris Canonici* (2. ed., 5 vols., Taurini: Marietti, 1936-1947), I, 367.

[2] Barbosa, *Iuris Ecclesiastici Universi Libri Tres* (Lugduni, 1660), Lib. II, cap. I, n. 26; Rossi, *op. cit.*, p. 60.

[3] Vermeersch-Creusen, *Epitome Iuris Canonici* (6. ed., 3 vols., Mechliniae: H. Dessain, 1937-1946), I, 275; Beste, *Introductio in Codicem* (2 ed., Collegeville, Minnesota: St. John's Abbey Press, 1944), p. 225; Bouscaren-Ellis, *Canon Law, A Text and Commentary* (Milwaukee: Bruce, 1946), p. 151.

for they take into consideration only the territorial parish. The third, though, is all-inclusive, since it leaves room for the inclusion of all categories of parishes, the personal or family parishes as well as the mixed or national parishes. The personal or family parish lacks the element of territoriality completely, and membership in the parish results from a purely personal quality, such as rite, family, descent, duty or profession. A mixed parish is one in which the group of the faithful is determined by both personal and territorial criteria, but since the personal note is most commonly one of nationality, parishes of this type are generally called national parishes.[4]

Included under the generic term of "parish" are also the quasi-parishes, which likewise may be territorial, personal or mixed. They are essentially identical with the parish, differing only because of the different kind of hierarchical unit of which they form a part.[5] The quasi-parish is a part of a vicariate apostolic or of a prefecture apostolic, whereas the parish is a part of a canonically established diocese.[6]

B. *Constitutive*

Secondly, a consideration of the work "constitutive" is in order. It is defined as tending or assisting to constitute, and also (philos.) as entering into the nature as a formative element or necessary attribute.[7] According to its first meaning, an apt synonym for the word would be "accessory." An accessory element, then, is a major element that aids subordinately to constitute a parish, one that is usually present but not necessarily so. The writer is fully

---

[4] Beste, *loc. cit.;* Bouscaren-Ellis, *op. cit.*, p. 152; Cappello, *Summa Iuris Canonici* (3 vols., Vols. I-II, 4. ed., 1945; Vol. III, 3. ed., 1940, Romae: Apud Aedes Universitatis Gregorianae), II, 440.

[5] Coronata, *Institutiones Iuris Canonici*, I, 368, footnote n. 8.

[6] *Codex Iuris Canonici Pii X Pontificis Maximi iussu digestus Benedicti Papae XV Auctoritate promulgatus, praefatione, fontium annotatione et indice analytico-alphabetico ab Emo Petro Card. Gasparri auctus* (Romae: Typis Vaticanis, 1917; Reimpressio, Westminster, Maryland: The Newman Book Shop, 1946), canon 216, § 3. Hereafter simply the canon itself is cited.

[7] *Webster's New International Dictionary* (2. ed., Springfield, Mass.: Merriam Webster, 1931), s.v. *constitutive.*

aware that the word "accessory" in itself does not convey this full meaning. He realizes that the term in itself can be applied to the most minute elements which aid to make up the parochial institute, and so he has designedly added the clause, "a major element, usually present but not necessarily so," in order to delimit his study of the constitutive elements. This somewhat arbitrarily applied meaning is to be kept in mind in the perusal of this work.

In its philosophical connotation the word "constitutive" denotes something absolutely or inherently essential. Whilst one of the major purposes of this dissertation will be a treatment of the essential elements of the parish, yet an examination of the accessory elements will not be neglected.

ARTICLE 2. NORMS FOR DETERMINING THE ELEMENTS OF PARISHES

The norms for determining the constitutive elements of parishes can be taken only from ecclesiastical law. The legislation of the Church, however, is sometimes ambiguous and obscure. Especially is this true in relation to the constitutive elements of parishes. Nowhere in the Code is there found a clear enumeration of the elements required in the constitution of the parochial institute. Although Canon 216, § 1, serves as a description of the parish, it can hardly be termed a definitive indication of its constituents. How, then is one to decide what are the essential requirements in the formation of a parish? Perhaps they are best judged with the following used as bases: the decrees of the Church, customs having the force of law, the interpretations of these decrees and customs by the ecclesiastical tribunals and, finally, the interpretations rendered by the commentators, new and old.

While the opinions of the pre-Code commentators and the decisions of the ecclesiastical tribunals are of high worth, it has been decided to limit the consideration of the constitutive elements in this first chapter to an examination of the proposals of the more modern commentators. Perhaps some readers are inclined not to bear with this reversal of the ordinary procedure. They may expect to find the views of modern commentators aired in the concluding sections of a treatise. However, good reason is found for this unorthodox manner of presentation. A presentation of the matter in the accustomed style would be most difficult. The history of the parish is vague and confusing. At times the institute itself is beyond recognition, and so much more are its individual elements. Why, then, attempt a presentation of the matter as a whole? Added confusion would be the only result.

Certainly, for the sake of a more orderly development, an individual treatment accorded the components of the parish is much more desirable. Hence, required before the materialization of such a project can take place is at least a tentative decision on what these elements are. The plan of the writer, therefore, is to present at this point a summarized view of the post-Code commentators on the matter. Subsequent chapters will follow with a brief outline of the parochial institute in general and a more detailed historical treatment of the respective elements. The treatise will close with a canonical examination of the components.

A full realization is had that the opinions of the modern commentators cannot be completely divorced either from the prior decrees of the Church or from the proposals of the pre-Code commentators. The recent authors frequently serve merely as a mirror of the preceding legislation and opinion. That, however, is precisely a corroborative argument for a presentation of their views first.

ARTICLE 3. OPINION OF COMMENTATORS ON THE CONSTITUTIVE ELEMENTS

Although, as has been indicated, Canon 216 serves as nothing more than a description of parishes, modern commentators without exception use it as a basis for their enumeration of the constitutive elements. The Canon follows:

> **§ 1. Territorum cuiuslibet dioecesis dividatur in distinctas partes territoriales; unicuique autem parti sua peculiaris ecclesia cum populo determinato est assignanda, suusque peculiaris rector, tanquam proprius eiusdem pastor, est praeficiendus pro necessaria animarum cura.**

§ 2. Pari modo vicariatus apostolicus et praefectura apostolica, ubi commode fieri possit, dividantur.

§ 3. Partes dioecesis de quibus in § 1, sunt *paroeciae;* partes vicariatus apostolici ac praefecturae apostolicae, si peculiaris rector eisdem fuerit assignatus, appellantur *quasi-paroeciae.*

§ 4. Non possunt sine speciali apostolico indulto constitui paroeciae pro diversitate sermonis seu nationis fidelium in eadem civitate vel territorio degentium, nec paroeciae mere familiares aut personales; ad constitutas autem quod attinet, nihil innovandum, inconsulta Apostolica Sede.

Maroto (1875-1937), writing one year after the Code (1919), upon offering a concise definition of the parish,[8] stated that the notes or proper characteristics by which the nature of the parish is defined are three: 1—that it be a lesser and distinct part of some diocese or quasi-diocese; 2—that its purpose be the immediate and special care of souls; 3—that it have its own special church, a determinate people or *"coetus fidelium,"* and its own proper pastor assigned over them for the care of their souls. Maroto concluded with the statement that the notion of a determined territory may also be added, for it is usually found as an element in the canonical parish, but he denied territorial limits has any necessary place in the generic definition of a parish, since "there are other types of parishes that do not postulate the element of territory."[9]

Fanfani, writing three years later (1924), offered a minimum of comment on the matter, and simply listed the elements in the constitution of a parish as the following: 1—a territory, circumscribed by definite limits, which is a part of a diocese; 2—a group of the faithful living in said territory; 3—a proper priest,

---

[8] "Paroecia vel parochia ad sensum novi Codicis (cf. cc. 216 et 451) est in genere unaquaeque ex distinctis partibus minoribus in quas dividitur aliqua dioecesis vel quasi-dioecesis ad peculiarem et immediatam animarum curam gerendam, cum sua peculiari ecclesia assignata, determinato populo adscripto, suoque peculiari rectore, tamquam proprio eiusdem pastore, praefecto, qui sane peculiaris rector dicitur *parochus."—Institutiones Iuris Canonici* (2 vols., Matriti, 1918-1919), II, 137.

[9] *Op. cit.,* II, 138.

who has the care of souls. He stated however that, if a parish is to constitute an ecclesiastical benefice, a sufficient endowment (*congrua dos*) with all the formalities required by law must likewise obtain.[10]

Rossi (1932) enumerates a distinct territory, a determinate people, a parochial church and a proper pastor as the constitutive elements and concludes with a note that the ecclesiastical benefice does not pertain to the essence of a parish, since it is possible to erect a parish without a benefice. He thereby infers that the endowment is not to be listed as an element.[11]

Connolly (1938) offers little that is new in his analysis of the nature of the parochial institute. While adverting to the usual concepts of a community of the faithful, of a determinate territory (or by exception an exclusive classification or group of persons), and of a priest with the care of souls, he adds that a church is not strictly a component part, since a parish can be canonically established before the church has been built. Since, however, "it is usually comprised in the notion of a fully organized parish," he includes it in his enumeration of the constitutive elements.[12]

The four commonly accepted elements(a specified congregation, a determinate territory, a specific church and a proper resident pastor) receive mention by Ciesluk in his study on *National Parishes in the United States* (1944), but he proceeds to demonstrate that these four elements are not inherent requisites, that a parish can exist without any one of them. First of all, Canon 216, § 4, abstracts from all need of territorial limits. While designating the *coetus fidelium* and the pastor who ministers to their needs as the principal parts of the parochial institute, he still states that a parish could possibly exist without actual parishioners. The case, so Ciesluk writes, is more hypothetical than practical, and simply implies a temporary absence of people from the parochial district, e.g., in time of war or flood. The parish at

---

[10] *De Iure Parochorum ad Normam Codicis Iuris Canonici* (Romae, 1924), p. 3 (hereafter cited *De Iure Parochorum*).

[11] *De Paroecia*, p. 60.

[12] *The Canonical Erection of Parishes,* The Catholic University of America Canon Law Studies, n. 114 (Washington, D. C.: The Catholic University of America, 1938), p. 3.

that time simply reflects a passive existence as distinguished from the active function normally manifested.

One can, so the author continues, understand the pastoral office in the same way. During the absence of the pastor through death or removal, the parish does not thereby cease to exist as such, nor does the pastoral office disappear. Rather, it continues passive in its appearance until another pastor is appointed to fill the office. But apart from an act of canonical establishment, neither the presence of the people, nor that of the priest, nor the two taken jointly, would *ipso facto* point to the existence of a parish. In relation to the church as a constitutive element, Ciesluk cites Connolly, who asserts that parishes can be canonically established before the church has been built.

After describing the preceding elements as insufficient in themselves and as furnishing merely the material factors requisite for the establishment of a parish, Ciesluk proposes the question, "What, then, is the formal element required before a parish can be considered as canonically established?" He answers, "It seems that this formal element is the act of a competent ecclesiastical authority erecting the parish." He accordingly insists upon the absolute necessity of this act, but he concludes with the remark that a formal *decree* of erection is not necessary in and of itself.[13]

Mundy, in his study *The Union of Parishes* (1945) presents by far the best analysis of the constituent elements of parishes. His views are best presented in his own words:

> The constituent elements or proper characteristics of a parish . . . are, therefore, three:
>
> 1. A parish must constitute a distinct part of a diocese, whether the partition be made by reason of *territorial circumscription,* or whether it have as its basis the *personal characteristics* of the people who dwell therein, such as language, nationality, or diversity of rite.
>
> Many authors in discussing this point enumerate a distinct *territory* as a constituent part of a parish. Al-

---

[13] *National Parishes in the United States,* The Catholic University of America Canon Law Studies, n. 190 (Washington, D. C.: The Catholic University of America Press, 1944), pp. 3-6 (hereafter cited *National Parishes*).

though this is very often, indeed, in the majority of cases, true, yet it would seem incorrect to require a distinct *territory* in the generic definition of a parish. For a so-called "national" parish is just as much a parish in every sense of the word as is a territorial parish. Yet it may exist without any definite territorial circumscription whatsoever. Thus, for instance, in an exceedingly small diocese it could happen that all the persons of a certain nationality, language, or rite within that diocese would pertain to a particular national parish. Here there would be no parochial circumscription other than that of the diocese itself. Their limits would be identical. Notwithstanding this, the fact that these persons constitute a particular *part* or section of the diocese, not a particular *territory,* is sufficient to classify their parish as a true canonical parish in every sense of the word, all the other requisites, of course, being present.

2. This division of a diocese into separate parts must have as its special purpose (*ratio formalis*) the facilitating or fostering of the particular care of souls.

3. This particular section of the diocese must have the following material elements:

a. Every parish must have a church proper unto itself. It is not essential that the church be actually constructed at the time the parish is founded. There must, however, be present the intention of erecting a church, especially designated for this group of people. Some other edifice may be used in the meantime.

b. Every parish must have its own proper pastor. Again it is not essential that there be physically present at all times the person of the pastor himself. Accordingly, a parish does not cease to be a parish merely because its pastor has been transferred to another parish, or has, perhaps, died, and no other has as yet been appointed in his stead. It would be better, therefore, to state that it is the office of pastor rather than the person of the pastor himself which must be permanently established in every canonical parish.

c. Finally, every parish must have a determined group of people pertaining thereto. As already mentioned above, this determination may be made either by reason of the territory in which these people live, or by reason of their personal characteristics, such as language, nationality or rite. In the former case the inhabitants of this particular

> parish become parishioners by acquiring a domicile or quasi-domicile within the limits of the parish itself.[14]

An analysis of Mundy's views will show that he considers the *office* of pastor, which has for its purpose the care of souls, together with a determinate group of people as the absolutely essential elements in the constitution of a parish. He looks upon the church and a territory as accessory elements—usually present but not necessarily so. The substantiating arguments he presents in defense of his opinions are excellent. Yet Mundy leaves something essential untouched. First of all, he makes no mention of an endowment as an element in the establishment of a parochial institute. In the light of the fact that the author employs the entire second chapter of his work for establishing the doctrine that parishes are ecclesiastical benefices,[15] it seems strange that he abstracted from the notion of endowment as an equally essential element, for the endowment is as essential to a benefice as people are to a parish. It is true that, once a parish is established, it can lose its endowment and still continue in existence.[16] This contingency, however, is so exceptional, that the non-mention of endowment as an element seems to leave room for a misimpression. The notion of an endowment must be included at least among the accessory elements.

While Ciesluk's opinion, namely that a parish can exist without actual parishioners and without an active pastoral office, deals with hypothesis rather than with fact, yet his reasoning that an act of a competent ecclesiastical authority is absolutely necessary for the erection of a parish is entirely acceptable. Mundy foregoes all mention of this in his enumeration of the constitutive elements.

To summarize the matter, then, the writer proposes the following list of elements as constitutive of a parish: A determinate group of people, the office of pastor, and the act of a competent eccle-

---

[14] *The Union of Parishes,* The Catholic University of America Canon Law Studies, n. 204 (Washington, D. C.: The Catholic University of America Press, 1945), pp. 9-11.

[15] *Op. cit.,* pp. 20-41.

[16] Cappello, *Summa Iuris Canonici,* II, 514; cf. infra, chap. VII, art. 2.

siastical authority by means of which alone juridical existence can come to a parish. Among the accessory elements he includes territorial limits, a church, and its endowment. At this point he does not seek to offer any proof in defence of this enumeration, but he hopes in the succeeding chapters to furnish substantiation for the enumeration as here proposed.

ARTICLE 4. THE CLASSIFICATION OF PARISHES

Since reference will necessarily have to be made to the various kinds of parishes in the following chapters, a listing of these categories seems in place here.

a. *Parishes and quasi-parishes.* The distinction between parishes and quasi-parishes, as has already been stated, is one that is based upon the hierarchical unit of which they form a part. It would be a wrong notion to conceive of quasi-parishes as imperfect parishes. The Code itself considers them of equal rank with parishes which are strictly designated as such.[17]

b. *Territorial, personal and mixed parishes.* The distinction here applicable has already been considered, but a restatement seems warranted. A territorial parish implies a subdivision of the territory of a diocese with a proper pastor and a group of people pertaining thereto, so that membership in the parish is defined by reason of domicile or quasi-domicile. A personal parish is one that abstracts from territorial limits. For its people a definite membership is determined in connection simply with their personal qualities, that is, without respect to the consideration of territory. A mixed parish is one whose membership is determined by both personal and territorial criteria, e.g., a parish for all the Germans living within a specified territory.

c. *Independent and incorporated* parishes. An independent parish is one that exists in and of its own right; an incorporated parish is one that has been united to another ecclesiastical institute or office, either in temporalities alone, or in both temporalities and spiritualities.

d. *Parishes with movable and irremovable pastoral incum-*

[17] Canon 451, § 2, 1°.

bents. In the latter class of parishes there attaches to the tenure of the pastoral office both a subjective and an objective perpetuity. In the former class the pastoral office itself exists with objective perpetuity, but the incumbent holds the office with a lesser degree of subjective stability, so that his removal from his office can be effected through more lenient formalities of law.

e. *Secular and religious parishes.* The former pertain in *title* solely to the secular clergy, the latter to the religious clergy.

f. *Mother and daughter parishes.* This classification has a historical origin, the mother parish by reason of convention and custom claiming certain rights which the daughter parish (without losing its identity as a true parish) had to bestow as a token of honor.

CHAPTER II

A Brief Outline of Parochial Development and a Historical Synopsis of the Constitutive Elements From the Origin of the Parish to the Council of Trent (1545-1563)

ARTICLE 1. A BRIEF OUTLINE OF PAROCHIAL DEVELOPMENT

In granting the power of authority over His church, Christ addressed the Apostles in these words: "All power in heaven and earth has been given to Me. Go, therefore, and make disciples of all nations, baptizing them in the name of the Father, and of the Son and of the Holy Spirit, teaching them to observe whatsoever I have commanded."[1] An accumulation of this power is found, as in a derivative source, in the Roman Pontiff.[2] However, as an aid in this mission the episcopacy was instituted by divine authority. The bishops, dependent upon the Supreme Pontiff and guided by the Holy Spirit, were to be subordinate shepherds ruling a particular portion of the faithful.[3]

In ancient Christianity, therefore, the Church universal was by the will of Almighty God Himself divided among various bishops, who ruled under the supervision of the Roman Pontiff. When organization reached a progressive stage of development, this episcopal ruling authority was territorially limited to certain sections by the Apostles themselves, or at least upon command from the Apostles.[4] The bishop was the pastor of the whole diocese. He utilized the services of the priests and the deacons only when he himself was impeded in exercising the *cura animarum*.[5]

---

[1] Matth., XXVIII; 18.

[2] Coronata, *Institutiones Iuris Canonici,* I, 362.

[3] Acts, XX; 28: "Take heed to yourselves and to the whole flock in which the Holy Spirit has placed you as bishops, to rule the Church of God. . . ."

[4] Titus, I, 5; *Casus* ad c. 1, D. LXXX; Wernz-Vidal, *Ius Canonicum* (7 vols. in 8, Romae: Apud Aedes Universitatis Gregorianae, 1923-1938), II, n. 721.

[5] Rossi, *De Paroecia,* p. 10; Fanfani, *De Iure Parochorum,* p. 7.

Nowhere is there found the least indication that parishes (as in the present signification of the term) existed in the first three centuries.[6] But, with a decline in the intensity of the disastrous persecutions which afflicted the Church almost from the beginning, the missionary efforts of the early evangelists bore fruit. Conversions from paganism numbered into the thousands. No longer was the bishop able to cope with the changed situation through personal preaching and administration of the sacraments. A dire need was found for erecting new churches besides the cathedral churches, and of dividing the care of souls with the presbyters and deacons. In Rome itself in the middle of the third century twenty-five of these churches were erected *"propter baptismum et poenitentiam multorum qui convertebantur ex paganis, et propter sepulturas martyrum."*[7] These secondary churches, however, were never true and independent parochial churches; still one may regard them as the predecessor of the present parish church.[8]

It is most difficult to determine the precise year or, for that matter, the exact century to which can be ascribed the foundation of the parochial institute throughout the universe. In the East, perhaps the first indication of an incipient parish life outside the city is found about the middle of the fourth century in the See of Antioch, where rural functions were entrusted to the chorepiscopi.[9] A more complete development, however, is suggested in the Council of Chalcedon (451).[10]

[6] Thomassinus, *Vetus et Nova Ecclesiae Disciplina* (10 vols., Parisiis, 1688), Pars I, Lib. II, cap. XXI, n. 1 (hereafter cited Thomassinus).

[7] Thomassinus (Pars I, Lib. II, cap. XXI, n. 11) credited their erection to Pope St. Marcellus (304-309), but evidently in error, for in the *Liber Pontificalis* their creation is ascribed to Pope St. Dionysius (259-268). Cf. Duchesne, *Le* LIBER PONTIFICALIS, *Texte, Introduction et Commentaire* (2 vols., Paris, 1886-1892), I, 157 (hereafter cited *Le* LIBER PONTIFICALIS).

[8] Wernz, *Ius Decretalium* (6 vols., Romae, 1898-1905), II, n. 821; Ciesluk, *National Parishes*, p. 8.

[9] Council of Antioch (341), c. 8—Mansi, *Sacrorum Conciliorum Nova et Amplissima Collectio* (53 vols. in 60, Parisiis, 1901-1927), II, 1323 (hereafter cited Mansi).

[10] *Actio Decima Quinta*, c. 10—Hardouin, *Acta Conciliorum et Epistolae Decretales ac Constitutiones Summorum Pontificum* (12 vols., Parisiis, 1714-1715), II, 603 (hereafter cited as Hardouin).

In the West, parochial development was somewhat slower. An embryonic parish life is found rurally in Africa and in Spain in the fourth century, but it blossomed into maturity only a number of centuries later.[11] In Italy the secondary churches, already referred to, made their appearance in the countryside during the fifth century.[12] They were erected for the convenience of the people by the bishop, or by the lords on their estates, or by the monasteries.[13]

Originally they were mere oratories for the singing of hymns and for the united recitation of prayers. At a later time the *cura animarum* was committed to clerics resident at these chapels and churches. Dependently on the bishop the clerics performed certain non-reserved sacred functions there. Soon in the more populous localities and on the larger estates the chapels came to be acknowledged as churches for the celebration of Mass.[14] Mass was said there on Sundays and holy days of obligation. Increasingly the chapels took on the appearance of self-sufficient parochial institutes. Not long thereafter they were grouped together according to locality, and each group was then placed under the supervision of a mother church, where baptism was administered solemnly at Easter and Pentecost by the resident priest (*archi-presbyter*).

It was this latter church that later came to be identified as the *ecclesia baptismalis*.[15] In 527 the Council of Carpentras indicated the tendency to complete the parochial status of these churches, both baptismal and minor rural, with a decree that all offerings

---

[11] Council of Carthage (390), c. 9—Mansi, III, 695; Council of Elvira (306), c. 21—Mansi, II, 9.

[12] *Epistola Leonis I*—Migne, *Patrologiae Cursus Completus, Series Latina* (221 vols., Parisiis, 1844-1864), LIV, 654 (hereafter cited *MPL*).

[13] Kurtscheid, *Historia Iuris Canonici: Historia Institutorum*, Vol. I (ab Ecclesiae Fundatione usque ad Gratianum) (Romae: Officium Libri Catholici, 1941), p. 166 (hereafter cited *Historia Institutorum*).

[14] Council of Agde (506), c. 21—Mansi, VIII, 328; Council of Auvergne (535), c. 15—Mansi, VIII, 862.

[15] Council of Auxerre (578), c. 20—Mansi, IX, 914. Cf. Waldron, *The Minister of Baptism*, The Catholic University of America Canon Law Studies, n. 170 (Washington, D. C.: The Catholic University of America Press, 1942), p. 30.

were to be expended on the church itself, and for the support of the pastoral incumbent (*archi-Presbyter* or *presbyter dioecesanus.*)[16]

Besides these churches there arose others which may be described as oratories or chapels. They had no resident clerics, but on certain days the presbyters of the major churches or other episcopal delegates performed the sacred functions. Generally of the same nature were the oratories erected on the larger estates. The manorial church, however, was at times of a parochial character.[17]

The evolution of the parish within Rome and Alexandria was somewhat parallel to the development in the countryside,[18] but in the other cities it unfolded much more gradually. Indeed, it was not until the ninth and tenth centuries, but with the two exceptions, that urban parishes came into existence.[19] However, much difficulty attends any effort which seeks to determine the exact status of these parishes. An examination of the *Decree* of Gratian and of the Decretal Collections sheds only a meager light. A partial clarification of the juridical status of parochial institutes was begun with the Council of Trent.

ARTICLE 2. A HISTORICAL SYNOPSIS OF THE CONSTITUTIVE ELEMENTS FROM THE ORIGIN OF THE PARISH TO THE COUNCIL OF TRENT (1545-1563)

A. *Territorial Limits*

Territorial limits have been defined as fixed boundaries or lines of demarcation by means of which one district or locality became distinguished from another. Usually it was some stone

---

[16] Hardouin, II, 1095.

[17] IV Council of Orleans (541), c. 26—Mansi, IX, 117.

[18] Bouix, *Tractatus de Parocho*, p. 33.

[19] Contrary to the contentions of Wernz (*Ius Decretalium,* II, n. 821), of Fanfani (*De Iure Parochorum,* p. 4) and of many others, Schaefer (+ 1948) seems to have proved conclusively that there existed city parishes in the ninth and tenth centuries. Cf. *Pfarrkirche und Stift im deutschen Mittelalter,* Kirchenrechtliche Abhandlungen hrsg. von U. Stutz, 3. Heft (Stuttgart, 1903), pp. 23-28.

markers, mountains, rivers or streams that served to establish a dividing line between the adjacent or neighboring districts.[20]

The exact historical origin of the drawing of territorial limits for the parish is most difficult to determine. Little is found either in Gratian or in the Decretal Law, and the commentators remained almost completely silent on this point. Rufinus (+ 1190), who wrote ca. 1158,[21] and Hostiensis (+ 1271), who wrote in the middle of the thirteenth century,[22] stated that the first institution of parishes and the initial division of the diocese took place in Rome under Pope Dionysius (259-268). But perhaps, as Schmalzgrueber (1663-1735) taught, Pope Dionysius only restored the division which already had been made before his time.[23] These authors founded their assertions on c. 1, C. XIII, q. 1,[24] which, though pseudo-Isidorian,[25] was certainly based on a text contained in the *Liber Pontificalis:* "Dionysius . . . presbyteris ecclesias dedit et cymiteria et parrochias dioecesis constituit."[26]

Van Espen (1646-1728), having rejected this supposed letter of Pope Dionysius (c. 1, C. XIII, q. 1), subscribed to the opinion that a territorial division of the diocese into parishes took place

---

[20] Pirhing, Lib. III, tit. 29, n. 9; Schmalzgrueber, *Ius Ecclesiasticum Universum* (5 vols. in 12, Romae, 1843-1845), Lib. III, tit. 29, n. 21 (hereafter cited with the use of the author's name).

[21] *Die Summa Decretorum des Magister Rufinus* (ed. Heinrich Singer, Paderborn, 1902), p. 305.

[22] *Summa Aurea* (Venetiis, 1570), Lib. III, tit. 29, n. 1.

[23] *Ius Ecclesiasticum Universum,* Lib. III, tit. 29, n. 21.

[24] (*Dionysius Episcopus Severo Episcopo*)—"Ecclesias singulas singulis presbyteris dedimus; parrochias et cimiteria eis divisimus, et unicuique ius proprium habere statuimus, ita videlicet, ut nullus alterius parrochiae terminos aut ius invadat, sed unusquisque terminis suis sit contentus, et taliter ecclesiam et plebem sibi commissam custodiat, ut ante tribunal aeterni iudicis ex omnibus sibi commissis rationem reddat, et non iudicium sed gloriam pro suis actibus percipiat."—Jaffé, *Regesta Pontificum Romanorum ab condita Ecclesia ad annum post Christum natum MCXVIII* (2. ed., correctam et auctam auspiciis Gulielmi Wattenbach curaverunt S. Löwenfeld, F. Kaltenbrunner, P. Ewald, 2 vols., Lipsiae, 1885-1888), I, n. CIXL (hereafter cited Jaffé).

[25] Hinschius, *Decretales Pseudo-Isidorianae et Capitula Agilramni* (Lipsiae, 1863), p. 196.

[26] Duchesne, *Le* LIBER PONTIFICALIS, I, 157.

in Alexandria in the fourth century. He offered as sole testimony a weak argument derived from St. Athanasius' *Apologia contra Arianos.*[27]

Although the *"fines parochiarum"* were often referred to in the *Decree* of Gratian,[28] the canons were generally applicable to diocesan limits exclusively.[29] There is one doubtful canon, however,[30] which tends to support Kurtscheid's (1877-1941) contention that territorial limits were becoming more and more common in the fifth century.[31] Yet the lack of distinct canonical references in Gratian is puzzling, and it stands as a hindrance to a definite solution of the problem.

Stutz (1868-1938) contended that the apportionment of diocesan territory into parishes began its development through the sole influence of the proprietary church. With the pseudo-Isidorian text as based on the *Liber Pontificalis* in mind, and in the light of Kurtscheid's contention, one finds it difficult to accept his view. Nevertheless, his theory is worth repeating. It is best stated in his own words.

> (In pre-Germanic times) there were already, of course, many churches in existence, particularly in country districts, besides the episcopal church; but in spiritual matters they were simply subordinate chapels of the episcopal church, and from the point of view of the law of property they were owned by the bishopric and were subject, together with the revenues derived from them, to the bishop's arbitrary administration, limited only by the prohibition of alienation. . . .
>
> With the entry of Germanic peoples into the Church,

[27] *Jus Ecclesiasticum Universum* (ed. novis., 10 vols. in 5, Venetiis, 1789), Tom. I, pars I, tit. II, cap. I, n. 2.

[28] Cf. cc. 4-7, C. XVI, q. 3, and cc. 1, 3, C. IX, q. 2.

[29] *Glossa* ad c. 5, C. XVI, q. 3, s.v. *parrochias.*

[30] C. 54, C. XVI, q. 1 reads: "Plures baptismales ecclesiae in una terminatione esse non possunt, sed una tantummodo cum capellis suis. . . ." But the origin of this canon is most uncertain. Nothing definite can be decided concerning it. Gratian attributed it to a Council of Toledo, but the *Correctores Romani* to a Council of Aix-la-Chapelle. The Friedberg edition of the *Decretum Gratiani* simply labelled it as of uncertain origin.

[31] *Historia Institutorum,* I, 167.

however, this situation was completely changed. Immediately the episcopal power found itself faced by a dangerous opponent. This opponent was the Germanic conception of territorial or manorial proprietorship (*Grundherrschaft*). And the object over which bishop and territorial magnates struggled, the point over which episcopal and seignorial interests conflicted, was the "proprietary church."

On the lands of a prosperous German stands a church. . . . The powers derived from public law . . . gave the manorial lord full direction and control over the church; he appointed and dismissed the priest, and the latter administered the church and exercised his office on the lord's behalf. . . .

After the end of the seventh and the beginning of the eighth century . . . private or proprietary churches sprang up everywhere. . . . For the Church, the bishop remained as he always had been, the sole possessor of administrative authority, church government continued to be regarded as centralized in character. Yet . . . it still remains undeniable that the church's unity, even in matters of ecclesiastical government, was by this time seriously menaced.

The situation was not without influence over the course of legal development. The bishop, had he retained his former omnipotence, would never have considered the possibility of regulating his legal relations with the subordinate clergy; for that would have been tying his own hands. For the bishop who was almost powerless, on the other hand, it was of the highest importance to know that his position in relation to the single churches and their ministers was legally safeguarded. For this reason, the period in question saw the beginning of a process which had been hitherto neglected: *the systematic, legal construction and delimitation of the diocese*. . . . As soon as each particular subordinate office was adequately strengthened, the office-holder himself could be depended on to maintain and further his own rights, and lay support and control then became unnecessary. *From that moment the time for the final shaping of the diocese had arrived;* for a bishopric was now possible in which a balance of power between a legally controlled central authority and a number of local authorities with

> many guaranteed rights could be maintained by purely ecclesiastical means. Such a bishopric was created in post-Germanic times. But the diocese of classical and modern canon law is nevertheless the daughter of the Germanic diocese.[32]

All dispute left aside, it is certain that parochial territorial limits were a juridic actuality at least by the eighth century.[33] But, even as late as the twelfth century the practice of fixing such limits had not become universal. This can be proposed with certitude, for the glossator on *Quod priori,* a dictum of Gratian on c. 1, C. XIII, q. 1, seemed to take it for granted that parishes could lack having boundaries: *"Sed si parochia non est limtata . . . ."*

In the Decretals of Gregory IX (1234) the few references to circumscribed limits for parishes are rather vague. Under the names of Popes Urban III (1185-1187) and Celestine III (1191-1198) decrees were issued concerning the inability of claiming praedial tithes from those who had transferred their parochial domicile[34] and regarding the non-prescriptibility of parochial boundaries,[35] but, as in Gratian, the legislation seemed exclusively to refer to diocesan boundaries. It is only through the doctrine of a later commentator[36] and a glossator[37] that one defi-

[32] Stutz, "The Proprietary Church as an Element of Medieval Germanic Ecclesiastical Law," *Studies in Medieval History, Medieval Germany (911-1252),* translated by Geoffrey Barraclough (2 vols., Oxford: Blackwell, 1938), II, 40-51 (hereafter cited The *Proprietary Church*). Italics inserted.

[33] Capitula Ecclesiastica (810-813), c. 10: "Ut terminum habeat unaquaque ecclesia, de quibus villis decimas recipiat."—*Monumenta Germaniae Historica* (188 vols. incomplete, Hannoverae, 1826—), Leges in 4, Sectio II (*Capitularia Regum Francorum*), Tom. I (ed. Alfredus Boretius, Hannoverae, 1883), 178 (hereafter cited *MGH*). Cf. also the Council of Tribur (895), c. 14—Mansi, XVIII, 139.

[34] C. 5, X, *de parochiis et alienis parochianis,* III, 29; Jaffé, n. 16457.

[35] C. 4, X, *dc parochiis et alienis parochianis,* III, 29; Jaffé, n. 15440.

[36] Gonzalez-Tellez (+ after 1673) explained that, misleading as the legislation of Urban III might be, it was meant also for parishes in the strict and proper sense. Cf. *Commentaria Perpetua in Singulos Textus Quinque Libros Decretalium Gregorii* IX (5 vols. in 4, Venetiis, 1699), Lib. III, tit. 29, caput finale, n. 5.

[37] *Casus* ad c. 4, X, *de parochiis et alienis parochianis,* III, 29: "In canonibus reperitur, limites provinciarum sive dioecesium, et ea quae limitibus adhaerent,

nitely finds these earlier laws accounted as applicable to parish limits as well.

In the fifteenth century there no longer was any question regarding the common existence of parochial boundaries. Reflected in the work of Panormitanus (1386-1453) is indisputable evidence that parishes which lacked limits constituted a juridical exception.[38]

B. *Group of the Faithful*

Constituting the principal part of the parochial institute together with the office of pastor was the *coetus fidelium.* A church without a group of the faithful could not constitute a parish in any but a hypothetical case.[39] Commentators generally omitted this as a point of discussion, but gave a thorough consideration to the following question: What minimum number of souls had to be postulated if a church was still to be regarded as having a *coetus fidelium?*

With unanimity reference was made to canon 5 of the XVI Council of Toledo (693), in which it was stated that the minimum requirement was ten *mancipia* and that, if a lesser number was found, the people were to be assigned to some neighboring church.[40] Relative to a determination of its proper meaning the

---

non praescribuntur; quaesitum fuit, utrum idem sit iudicium in limitibus parochiarum? Respondet, Idem servandum est in utroque. . . . Idem iuris est in minori quod in maiori."

[38] *Commentaria in Quinque Libros Decretalium* (8 vols., Venetiis, 1588). Lib. III, tit. 29, n. 1 (hereafter cited *Commentaria*).

[39] Boehmer (*Jus Parochiale* [Halae, 1760], sect. III, cap. III, n. 17) mentioned the possibility of the existence of a parish apart from any parishioners, but he simply contemplated the case that could occur in time of war, famine, etc., when, to escape danger, the faithful moved far from their parochial domicile. Cf. Ciesluk, *National Parishes,* p. 5.

[40] ". . . sed et hoc necessarium instituere duximus, ut plures ecclesiae uni nequaquam committantur presbitero, quia solus per totas ecclesias nec officium valet persolvere, nec rebus earum necessariam curam impendere, ea scilicet ratione cipimus, ut ecclesia, quae usque ad decem habuerit mancipia, super se habet sacerdotem, quae vero minus aliis coniungatur ecclesiis. Si quis sane episcoporum hanc nostram institutionem parvipenderit, duorum mensium spatio se noverit excommunicatione mulctari."—c. 3, C. X, q. 3.

word *mancipia* presents an almost insuperable difficulty. It seems altogether unlikely that the Fathers of the Council empoyed the term in its classical signification of slaves.[41] The glossator apparently held the opinion that the word meant ten individual persons, although this is not indisputably clear from the short text.[42] The *casus* on the canon, however, seemed to leave no question that ten persons were meant.[43] Again in the gloss to c. 1, X, *de electione electi potestate,* I, 6, *populus* was described as ten persons.[44] On the other hand, Rufinus (+ 1190), in commenting upon this canon, defended the theory that *mancipia* meant ten families or homes regardless of the number of inhabitants dwelling in it.[45]

Thus the opinion regarding the number of the faithful required for the constituting of a parish was divided, and no definitive solution for the problem seems possible in the pre-Tridentine period.

C. *The Office of Pastor*

A third and most important element in the constitution of a parish was the pastoral office, through which the *cura animarum* was to be exercised over a group of the faithful. One naturally inquires: "In what did the office of pastor consist? Were the spiritual administrations of the pastor taken singly, ever constitutive elements of the parish?

Since the parochial institute and the office of pastor are of human origin,[46] an objective evolution can readily be admitted. It has already been pointed out that in the early Church the litur-

---

[41] Schmalzgrueber, Lib. III, tit. 29, n. 7. Cf. Leage, *Roman Private Law* (2. ed., by C. H. Ziegler, London: Macmillan, 1932), p. 96, for classical meaning.

[42] *Glossa* ad c. 3, C. X, q. 3, s.v. *mancipia*: "Cum ergo decem faciant plebem. . . ."

[43] *Casus* s.v. *Unio*: ". . . ecclesia quae habet x parochianos, habeat proprium sacerdotem. . . ."

[44] *Glossa* s.v. *duo:* "Et decem homines faciunt populum. . . ."

[45] *Die Summa Decretorum des Magister Rufinus,* p. 305.

[46] Thomassinus, Pars I, Lib. II, cap. XXIII, n. 2; Bouix, *Tractatus de Parocho* (3 ed., Parisiis, 1880), p. 43.

gical functions were performed by the bishop, either personally or through a priest who acted in his stead. At a later time the numerous conversions to Christianity brought about the inefficiency of this method of spiritual care. Small chapels were erected in Rome *propter baptismum et poenitentiam multorum qui convertebantur ex paganis, et propter sepulturas martyrum.* Soon afterwards, when chapels were erected also in the countryside, the Eucharist was administered there.[47] Although at the beginning these chapels did not constitute parochial churches, and the priests in charge could not as yet be designated as pastors (for they still acted in the name of the bishop), yet an advance indication was given of the spiritual duties that were eventually to fall to the pastor *ex officio:* baptism, penance, burial, the offering of the Sacrifice and the administration of the Eucharist.

A complete historical examination of the development of these and other rites into parochial functions is beyond the scope of this dissertation.[48] Yet the writer feels obliged to indicate at least the beginnings of these duties as parochial functions. Especially is this true with regard to the sacrament of baptism, the administration of which at one time was exclusively parochial, and thus seemed to figure as an essential element in the constitution of the parish. Accordingly the first section of this article will deal solely with that sacrament, while the second will treat of the remaining functions.

1. The Administration of Baptism

Although the administration of private baptism had early become a presbyteral function,[49] solemn baptism was regularly performed in the Paschal season only by the archpriest—the resident presbyter of an *ecclesia baptismalis,* which held the distinction of being the mother church over a group of local rural churches.[50]

---

[47] Rossi, *De Paroecia,* p. 10.

[48] For a complete development, cf. Kelly, *The Functions Reserved to Pastors,* The Catholic University of America Canon Law Studies, n. 250 (Washington, D. C.: The Catholic University of America Press, 1947), pp. 5-27.

[49] Roman Synod (402), c. 7—Mansi, III, 1137.

[50] Waldron, *The Minister of Baptism,* p. 30.

The erection of baptistries in monasteries was forbidden, and from this it may be inferred that their erection was likewise forbidden in all other churches save the episcopal cathedral.[51] Yet the archpriest enjoyed his right only through a delegation *ad actum* by the bishop, for even in the sixth and seventh centuries there was legislation which insisted that priests should not baptize solemnly unless the bishop was impeded or had given his permission.[52]

As time went on, however, there was a general unwillingness on the part of the people to defer baptism until the paschal season, as was indicated by the II Council of Macon (585).[53] This brought it about that by the middle of the seventh century priests became ordinary ministers of solemn baptism,[54] and partially through the influence of the "proprietary church" system as obtaining in the Frankish Empire the exclusive right to administer this sacrament was finally reserved to the parish priest.[55] Just as the proprietors of the ancient estates were able to enforce the monopoly of their mills (force their tenants to take their grain to be ground in no mill but that of the lord of the estate), so, in exactly the same way, the bishop used his administrative authority in favor of the owner to forbid the parishioners to go for their spiritual needs to any but the domanial parish church.

At the end of the ninth century even the minor rural churches possessed baptismal fonts,[56] and so definitely parochial was the

---

[51] Decree of Gregory the Great (593)—Jaffé, n. 1261. (Gratian listed this decree under c. 7, C. XVIII, q. 2, but falsely attributed it to Pope Gelasius I [+ 496]).

[52] Capitula collecta a Martino Epis. Bracarensi, cc. 52, 53—Mansi, IX, 856; Council of Seville (619), c. 7—Mansi, X, 559.

Kurtscheid (*Historia Institutorum,* I, 167) cited the Council of Auxerre (578), c. 18 (Mansi, IX, 913) as evidence that the archpriest was the ordinary minister of baptism even at that time, but the final qualifying clause of the canon seems to argue contrariwise: "et quicumque presbyter ipsos (fideles) extra nostrum permissum recipere praesumpserit, tribus mensibus a communione ecclesiae sequestratur est."

[53] C. 3—Mansi, IX, 951. Cf. *MGH, Leges in 4,* Sectio III (*Concilia*), Tom. I (ed. F. Maassen, 1893), 166.

[54] IV Council of Toledo (633), c. 6—Mansi, X, 618.

[55] Stutz, *The Proprietary Church,* pp. 54-55.

[56] Waldron, *The Minister of Baptism,* p. 33.

possession of the font that the lack of it indicated the non-existence of a parish church.[57] It is precisely at this period in history that the possession of the right to administer baptism must be considered an essential element in the constitution of a parish.

In the city, up to that time, the cathedral, administered by the archpriest, remained the one and only parochial church, and in consequence possessed exclusive urban rights in regard to baptism.[58] Of the additional churches which were built in the cities some had baptistries. But the cathedral church did not forfeit its baptismal rights over the parishioners at whose churches there were no baptismal fonts, and it continued to possess a cumulative right for the bestowal of baptism in the event that the other churches had a baptismal font of their own.[59] As the number of urban parishes with baptistries increased, however, and as legislation which emphasized the exclusive right of the pastor to baptize his own subjects became more common,[60] the effect was noted by the archpriest and the cathedral chapter. Consequently, in an effort to regain their declining prestige, they sought to restrict the exercise of parochial powers by the priests stationed at the minor churches, in which the agencies of legal prescription and custom had vindicated the use of such powers.

With the development of new parishes in the country, the same exclusive competence was claimed by the mother church over the filial. That many cathedrals and mother churches were sustained in their contentions through many centuries is deducible from numerous post-Tridentine decrees.[61]

2. The Administration of the Other Sacraments; Further Parochial Rights

One cannot point to any definite date as marking the inception of each of these functions as parochial. It has been shown that the

[57] Houwen, *De Parochorum Statu,* Dissertatio Historico-Canonica (Lovanii, 1848), p. 51.

[58] Wernz, *Ius Decretalium,* II, n. 821.

[59] Kurtscheid, *Historia Institutionum,* I, 282.

[60] Ecclesiastical Laws of King Edgar (967), c. 15—Mansi, XVIII A, 515; Council of Poitiers (1100), c. 11—Mansi, XX, 1124.

[61] Cf. *infra,* Chapter III, footnote n. 43.

administration of baptism became a parochial right early in the history of the Church. Just when the administration of the other sacraments took on a parochial character is hard to determine. Unknown, too, is the full manner in which there evolved such other rights which ultimately pertained to the office of a pastor.

Although the priests in charge at the rural chapels, and at Roman and Alexandrian *tituli* in the early part of the fifth century, had the faculties of saying Mass[62] and of administering the sacraments of the Holy Eucharist, of penance and of baptism *ad nutum episcopi,*[63] the exclusive parochial character of these functions was not yet established, nor did the priest as yet perform these functions *ex officio.*[64]

The legislation which constrained parishioners to attend to their spiritual needs in their parish church appeared in the early sixth century when the Council of Agde (506) decreed:

> Si quis etiam extra parochias, in quibus legitimus est ordinariusque conventus, oratorium habere voluerit, reliquis festivitatibus, ut ibi Missas teneat, propter fatigationem familiae iusta ordinatione permittimus. Pasca vero, Natale Domini, Epiphaniam, Ascensionem, Pentecosten et Natale S. Joannis Baptistae, vel si qui maximi dies in festivitatibus habentur, non nisi in civitativus aut in parochiis teneant.[65]

One will note, however, that this decree did not prescribe any obligatory attendance in one's own parish church; it prescribed the attendance *in civitatibus aut in parochiis.* Perhaps the first unquestionable prescription in favor of the parish church is found in the Capitularies of Theodulf (ca. 798), Bishop of Orleans (+ 821),[66] which forbade priests to celebrate Mass at the same time that the Sacrifice was being offered in the parish churches,

---

[62] Innocentius I (401), *Ep. ad Decentium,* c. 5—Mansi, III, 1030.

[63] Roman Synod (402), c. 7—Mansi, III, 1137. Cf. Rossi, *De Paroecia,* p. 11.

[64] Perhaps the first pastoral right exercised *ex officio* by these priests was that of preaching and of public instruction. Cf. the II Council of Vaison (529), c. 2: "Non solum in civitatibus sed in omnibus parochiis verbum faciendi damus presybteris potestatem."—Mansi, VIII, 726.

[65] C. 21—Mansi, VIII, 328.

[66] C. 45—Mansi, XIII, 1006. Cf. also c. 14 of the same capitularies.

for it was there that the people fulfilled their obligation, and they were not to be withdrawn from attendance.[67] Decrees from which can be inferred an obligatory attendance at one's own parish church were issued by councils during the succeeding centuries,[68] and so forceful did the legislation become that Panormitanus (+ 1453) could state that any non-parishioner who out of contempt for his own pastor wished to hear Mass in another parish church could be ejected physically.[69]

In like manner, between the ninth and the thirteenth centuries restrictions were placed on the parishioners regarding the reception of penance, of Holy Comumnion, of Viaticum, and of extreme unction, and regarding the place for the celebration of marriage and also the place for the bestowal of Christian burial.[70] As with baptism, this was no doubt due at least in part to the influence of the proprietary church sytem. It seems reasonable to agree on this point with Stutz, who explained the matter as follows:

> The territorial magnates . . . wished to get some guarantee of permanence for their private churches. This led to the further development of parochial rights and parochial law. Purely ecclesiastical and public considerations had led to the introduction of the parish system.

[67] The Council of Nantes (alleged by some to have been held in 658 or 660) enacted a like prescription in canon 1. But modern research has indicated the very doubtful existence of the council. Cf. Fournier-Le Bras, *Histoire des Collections Canoniques en Occident depuis les Fausses Decretales jusqu'au Decret de Gratien* (2 vols., Paris: Recueil Sirey, 1931-1932), I, 259. The cited decree of this doubtful council is found in Mansi, XVIII A, 166, and in Gratian under c. 4, C. IX, q. 2.

[68] Council of Chalon-sur-Saone (813), c. 19: "Familiae vero ibi dent decimas suas, ubi infantes eorum baptizantur, et ubi per totum anni circulum missas audiunt."—Mansi, XIV, 100; Diet and Synod of Szabolcs (1092), c. 11—Mansi, XX, 763.

[69] *Commentaria,* Lib. III, tit. 29, cap. II, n. 2.

[70] Capitularies of Louis II (845-850), c. 11: ". . . quidam autem laici, qui vel in propriis vel in beneficiis suas habent basilicas, contempta episcopi dispositione non ad ecclesias, ubi baptismum et praedicationem et impositionem manus et alia Christi sacramenta percipiunt, decimas suas dant. . . ."—*MGH,* Leges in 4, Sectio II (*Capitularia Regum Francorum*), Tom. II (ed. A. Boretius et V. Krause, Hannoverae, 1890), 82-83; Council of Chalon-sur-Saone (813), c. 19—Mansi, XIV, 100; Rule of Chrodegang (c. 9)—*MPL,* IXC, 1072; Letter of Amolo, Bishop of Lyons (850)—*MPL,* CXVI, 75.

> For the purpose of ecclesiastical organization smaller cures of souls had been set up within the bishop's sphere of action; for the sake of ecclesiastical order the faithful had been urged, if possible every Sunday and at least on the main festivals, to attend divine service in the parish church. Now, however, under the domination of the proprietary church regime, fiscal and private considerations came to the fore. In the course of time the lord was able to enforce the monopoly of his mill: by means of jurisdiction placed in his hands the wielder of the secular authority, who was often the local lord himself, could prohibit the inhabitants of a particular district from taking their corn to be ground in any but the seignorial mill. In exactly the same way, however, it was possible to get the bishop to use his administrative authority to forbid the parishioners to go for their spiritual needs to any but domanial parish church. And this was what happened. The parish churches, at first the proprietary ones and then those under the bishop's control, acquired a monopoly, and so there arose a body of parochial law, which in its legal character was—and where it has persisted until today, still is—neither more nor less than a medieval, Germanic assumption of the right of jurisdiction.[71]

Whereas most of the restrictions regarding the reception of the sacraments and the place for burial were at the beginning the legislation of local councils and bishops, they became official and universal church law with their inclusion in the Decretals of Gregory IX (1234)[72] in the *Liber Sextus* of Boniface VIII (1298),[73] and in the *Clementinae* (1317).[74]

---

[71] *The Proprietary Church,* pp. 54-55.

[72] C. 12, X, *de poenitentiis et remissionibus,* V, 38: "Omnis utriusque sexus fidelis, postquam ad annos discretionis pervenerit, omnia sua solus peccata saltem semel in anno confiteatur fideliter proprio sacerdoti . . . suscipiens reverenter ad minus in Pascha Eucharistiae sacramentum."

[73] C. 3, *de sepulturis,* III, 12, in VI°: "Is qui habet domicilium in civitate vel castro, quandoque ad villam se transfert recreationis causa, vel ut ruralia exerceat in eadem, si non electa sepultura decedat ibidem, non in ecclesia dictae villae, sed in sua parochiali . . . sepeliri debebit."

[74] C. 1, *de privilegiis et excessibus privilegiatorum* V, 7, in Clem.: "Religiosi, qui clericis aut laicis sacramentum unctionis extremae vel Eucharistiae ministrare, matrimoniave solemnizare, non habita super his parochialis

Panormitanus (+ 1453) summarized the legislation of the preceding general and local councils in answer to his question:

> In quo constat ius parochiale?
> I—Ut parochiani diebus festivis audiant Missam in parochia.
> II—Ut sacramenta percipiantur in hac ecclesia parochiali, seu a presbytero parochiae, et ut parochianus ibi sepeliatur.[75]

Although regulations on the administration of the sacraments, on attendance at Mass, and regarding the place of burial were thus enacted in favor of the parish, it nevertheless does not seem warranted to assert that these parochial prerogatives constituted essential elements in the constitution of a parish. At no one time (with the exception in the ninth century of the right to confer baptism) could it be asserted that a church did not enjoy parochial status for the reason that it did not possess some particular rights. This was so, for, despite the general law to the contrary, privileges regarding these prerogatives (as with baptism) were gained through legal prescription and customary usage by the cathedral and mother churches. Moreover, the picture of what constituted a church which enjoyed parochial status was further obscured by the countless apostolic privileges that were granted to the Mendicant Orders.[76] Yet possession of these rights undoubtedly served as an indication of the parochial status of a church.

D. *The Church Building*

A canonically established parish without the existence of a proper parish church is only a post-Tridentine development.[77] The earliest

presbyteri licentia speciali . . . praesumpserint, excommunicationis incurrant sententiam ipso facto."

[75] *Commentaria,* Lib. III, tit. 29, n. 2.

[76] *Bullarum Diplomatum et Privilegiorum Sanctorum Romanorum Pontificum Taurinensis Editio* (24 vols. et Appendix, Augustae Taurinorum, 1857-1872), V, 270 (hereafter cited *Bull. Rom.*); also *Bull. Rom.,* IV, 110; Gregorius IX, const., *Quoniam,* 10 maii 1227—Potthast, *Regesta Pontificum Romanorum inde ab anno post Christum natum MCXCVIII ad annum MCCCIV* (2 vols., Berolini, 1874-1875), n. 7896 (hereafter cited Potthast); c. 2, *de sepulturis,* III, 7, in Clem.— Potthast, n. 24913.

[77] S. C. C., *Feltrien.,* 15 iul. 1882—*Acta Sanctae Sedis* (41 vols., Romae, 1865-1908), XV (1882), 324 (hereafter cited *ASS*).

recorded legislation did not admit of such a conception. Historically the usual way rather was first to have the church and only then the parish. An examination of the Decree of Gratian impresses that fact indubitably upon the mind.[78] Especially impressive is c. 9, D. I, *de cons.* from which it can be assumed that one of the first requirements in the establishment of a parish was the erection of the church building.[79]

Decretal law closely followed this ancient tradition, but it was neither more nor less explicit than the preceding legislation. Especially worthy of note, however, is the letter of Pope Alexander III (1159-1181) to the Archbishop of York, in which among other things the erection of the church building was demanded before the division of the parish was to take place.[80]

Thus it seems that in the pre-Tridentine period the actual existence of the parish church must be recognized as an essential element for the constitution of a parish.

E. *Sufficient Endowment*

An examination of the early juridical sources reveals clearly that the Church, though not always insistent on a strict endow-

[78] C. 30, C. XII, q. 2 (Letter of Pope Gregory the Great to Augustine, Bishop of England (601): "Mos est apostolicae sedis ordinato episcopo praecepta tradere, ut de omni stipendio, quod accidit, quattuor debeant fieri portiones, una videlicet episcopo et familiae eius . . . alia clero, tertia pauperibus, quarta ecclesiis reparandis."—Jaffé, n. 1843; cf. c. 2, D. XXX; cc. 23, 26, 27, 28, C. XIII, q. 2; c. 3, C. X, q. 3; c. 45, C. XVI, q. 1.

[79] "Nemo ecclesiam aedificet antequam civitatis episcopus veniat, et ibidem crucem figat, publice atrium designet, et ante praefiniat, qui aedificare vult, quae ad luminaria, et ad custodiam, et stipendia custodum sufficiant, et ostensa donatione sic domum aedificet, et postquam consecrata fuerit, atrium eiusdem ecclesiae sancta aqua conspergat."

[80] "Ad audientiam nostram noveris pervenisse, quod villa, quae dicitur H., tantum perhibetur ab ecclesia parochiale distare, ut in tempore hiemali, quum pluviae, inundant, non possint parochiani sine magna difficultate ipsam adire, unde non valent congruo tempore ecclesiasticis officiis interesse. Quia igitur dicta ecclesia ita dicitur in reditibus abundare, quod praeter illius villae proventus minister illius convenienter valeat sustentationem habere, fraternitati tuae per apostolica scripta mandamus, quatenus, si res ita se habet, ecclesiam ibi aedifices, et in ea sacerdotem . . . instituas . . . ."—c. 3, X, *de ecclesiis aedificandis vel reparandis,* III, 48; Jaffé, n. 13884.

ment, has consistently demanded a sufficient means of support as a condition for the founding of a parish. As early as 601, Pope Gregory the Great, in a letter to Augustine, Apostle of England, instructed the latter on the manner in which he was to provide for the upkeep of the Church and the support of the clergy.[81] Even in the Novels of Justinian (ca. 540) the legislation provided that before he established a church the founder had to consult the bishop, and had at the same time to declare what he was willing to subscribe for the maintenance of the altar and the sustentation of the priest who was to be placed in charge.[82]

With the rise of the proprietary church, unmistakable demands for a strict endowment began to emerge. One *mansus*[83] was required for a church in the Capitularies of Louis the Pious (817),[84] and this later became universal ecclesiastical law with its adoption into the *Corpus Iuris Canonici.*[85]

It was one of the first concerns of Pope Alexander III (1159-1181) in his famous decree *Ad audientiam nostram* on the division of parishes that neither the mother church nor the newly created filial church should be without sufficient endowment.[86] Pope Innocent III (1198-1216) at the IV General Council of the Lateran (1215) reflected a similar concern when he wholeheartedly condemned patrons who supported the clerics in miserly fashion. He bitterly compained about the resultant lack of studiousness on the part of the clergy, and ordered that the priest in charge of a parish should receive a decent livelihood.[87]

---

[81] C. 30, C. XIII, q. 2—Jaffé, n. 1843; cf. cc. 55, 57, C. XVI, q. I.

[82] Nov. (68, 2). This law was later inserted in the *Decree* of Gratian. c. 9, D. I, *de cons.*

[83] Interesting is the glossator's explanation of this term s.v. *mansus* ad c. 1, X, *de censibus, exactionibus et procurationibus,* III, 39: "Mansus dicitur in vulgari Italicorum quantitas terrae, quae sufficit duobus bobus in anno laborandum"; cf. for further explanation Du Cange, *Glossarium ad Scriptores Mediae et Infimae Latinitatis* (6 vols., Parisiis, 1733), s.v. *Mansus.*

[84] C. 10—*MGH, Leges in 4,* Sectio II (*Capitularia Regum Francorum*) Tom. I (ed. Alfredus Boretius, Hannoverae, 1883), 277; cf. *Responsa Missis Data* (826), c. 2—*MGH, ibid.,* p. 314; cf. also *Capitularia de partibus Saxoniae* (775-790), c. 15 (*MGH, ibid.,* p. 69), in which two *mansi* were required.

[85] C. 1, X, *de censibus, exactionibus et procurationibus,* III, 39.

[86] C. 3, X, *de ecclesiis aedificandis vel reparandis,* III, 48.

[87] C. 20, X, *de praebendis et dignitatibus,* III, 5.

Subsequent local legislation stressed this Decretal law. In 1310 the Council of Cologne strictly prohibited the consecration of a church before certainty was had concerning a sufficient endowment.[88] There seems, then, hardly to be no doubt that the strict endowment had to be reckoned among the essential elements of the parish in the pre-Tridentine period.

F. *Permission of the Bishop*

That the permission of the bishop was required for the erection of the parish, and in earlier times (up to the sixth century) even for the performance of the individual priestly functions, was emphasized again and again in ecclesiastical law. Early restrictions prohibited priests, deacons or any others from doing anything without the special grant of the bishop. The priests were not to say Mass or to baptize unless they were specifically commanded to do so.[89]

The Council of Gangra (340/341) inflicted an excommunication on priests and people who, contemning the ecclesiastical sanctions, erected a church for themselves without the consent of the bishop.[90] And again in the Novels of Justinian consultation with the bishop was demanded.[91]

The creation of the pastoral office rendered void of course the legislation concerning episcopal permission for the individual priestly functions, but in the ninth century, with the emergence of the proprietary church system as a threat to the authority of the bishop, legislation demanding his consent for the erection of a parish once again became common.[92]

A demand for the consultation with the consent of the bishop

---

[88] C. 20; "Inhibemus, autem, ne aliqua ecclesia vel coemeterium, nisi dotatae . . . amodo consecrentur."—Mansi, XXV, 242.

[89] Cf. Bouix, *Tractatus de Parocho,* p. 20.

[90] C. 6: "Si quis praeter ecclesiam vult ecclesiam habere, et contemnens Ecclesiam vult ea quae sunt Ecclesiae agere, non conveniente presbytero de episcopi sententia, sit anathema."—Mansi, II, 1102.

[91] Nov. (68, 2).

[92] C. 44, C. XVI, q. 1: "Quicumque voluerit in sua proprietate ecclesiam aedificare, et consensum et voluntatem episcopi habuerit, in cuius parochia est, licitum fit. . . ." Cf. also the Council of Chalon-sur-Saone (813), c. 42—Mansi, XIV, 102.

was finally introduced into the universal law with a decree of the I General Council of the Lateran in 1123.[98] The lack of any subsequent similar legislation may well be an indication that the decree was strictly observed. Throughout this period the consent of the bishop is easily recognized as an absolutely essential element for the constitution of a parish.

---

[98] C. 7: "Nullus omnino archidiaconus, aut archipresbyter, sive prepositus, vel decanus animarum curam vel prebendas ecclesiae sine iudicio vel consensu episcopi alicui tribuat; immo, sicut sanctis canonibus constitutum est, animarum cura et pecuniarum ecclesiasticarum dispensatio in episcopi iudicio et potestate permaneat. . . ."—Mansi, XXI, 282. This legislation was incorporated by Gratian under c. 11, C. XVI, q. 7.

CHAPTER III

The Constitutive Elements of the Parish From the Council of Trent to the Present Code (1918)

ARTICLE I. PROVISIONS OF THE COUNCIL OF TRENT

A. *Territorial Limits and Group of the Faithful*

Hailed by many authors as an aid in clarifying the confusion regarding the constitutive elements of the parish was the famed decree of the Council of Trent (1545-1563) on parochial organization.

> In iis quoque civitatibus, ac locis, ubi parochiales ecclesiae certos non habent fines, nec earum rectores proprium populum, quem regant, sed promiscue petentibus sacramenta administrant, mandat sancta Synodus episcopo pro tutiori animarum eis commissarum salute, ut, distincto populo in certas propriasque parochias, unicuique suum perpetuum peculiaremque parochum assignet, qui eas cognoscere valeat, et a quo solo sacramenta suscipiant; aut alio utiliori modo, prout loci qualitas exegerit, provideant. Idemque in iis civitatibus ac locis, ubi nullae sunt ecclesiae parochiales quamprimum fieri curent; non obstantibus quibuscumque privilegiis et consuetudinibus, etiam immemorabilibus.[1]

Actually, however, in itself the decree does very little to eliminate the many vexing problems confronting the legal historian. First of all, the Fathers of the Council commanded the bishops to assign territorial limits to each parish. This, however, was not demanded as an absolutely essential requirement, for the Fathers referred to those churches as parochial which, prior to the Council, did not have distinct limits. Moreover territorial limits were to be established only as circumstances of place permitted. If a

[1] Sess. XXIV, *de ref.*, c. 13.

different but more suitable arrangement in assigning a distinct group of the faithful to a particular church presented itself, the bishops were not to hesitate in using it. Likewise, permanency of the pastor did not seem to be listed as an absolute requirement, for again, also dependent upon local circumstances, freedom was accorded to the bishops in the matter of carrying out this provision.

However, one cannot regard the decree as utterly without effect for determining the essential elements, although Bouix (1808-1870) tended to leave that impression. He even rejected as a resultant necessity the requirement that bishops find some means of assigning a *distinct* group of the faithful to a particular church. Bishops, according to him, were still at liberty, in accord with the suggestion of utility, to erect parishes where the sacraments could be administered indiscriminately (*promiscue*) to whosoever sought them. With that as his premise, he logically added that the Council, in demanding that the parishioners must have recourse to their pastors for the licit reception of the sacraments, did not urge this as an inflexible rule.[2]

Actually there was no freedom in either instance. A close scrutiny of the decree and a consideration of the previous jurisprudence,[3] as well as the legislation enacted in other sessions of the Council,[4] reveals that bishops had no choice; they were obliged to eliminate the practice whereby parish churches were without distinct groups of the faithful; and parishioners, except in rare circumstances, could receive the sacraments from none but their proper pastor.

The Council did not issue any instructions regarding the minimum number of people required as a material basis for the constituting of a parish, nor did it discard the previous doctrine on the matter. The long standing dispute, namely, whether the minimum requirement was ten persons or ten families, still remained.

B. *The Office of Pastor*

Among the many problems confronting the Council was the need for a declaration on the scope of the office of pastor. In the

---

[2] Bouix, *Tractatus de Parocho,* pp. 168-169.

[3] *Glossa* ad c. 2, *de sepulturis,* III, 7, in Clem., s.v. *Impendant.*

[4] Sess. XXIII, *de ref.,* c. 15; sess. XXIV, *de ref.,* c. 1.

course of time the pontifical concessions which had been granted the Mendicant Orders previous to the Council[5] developed by means of the existing system of reciprocal participation in them into an imposing array of privileges. Such was the resultant confusion in the ministry that the spiritual welfare of the faithful and, in some instances, the very existence of the parish church were endangered. A clarification of rights was deemed an urgent necessity.

Very important among the decrees was the curtailment of the wide powers to absolve, which previously had been granted to the religious. The Council commanded that no one, even though a regular, could hear the confessions of the laity unless he either held a parochial benefice or had after an examination received approbation from the bishop. All contrary privileges or customs were abolished.[6] To state that the power of the pastor over his parishioners was thereby greatly enhanced is superfluous. Yet this distinctive prerogative was short-lived. By the fact that the decree allowed the bishops to approve others than pastors for hearing confessions, it paved the way to the ultimate dissolution of that parochial right.

Further strengthening the prestige of the pastor was a reaffirmation of the decrees of the IV General Council of the Lateran (1215) concerning paschal Communion and confession in the parish church.[7] And beyond doubt the pastors, who repeatedly had reason for grievance when they saw the exercise of their rights relative to the administration of the sacrament of matrimony wantonly assumed by others, welcomed the decree *Tametsi,* which definitely required the presence of the pastor in the administration of this sacrament. The Council declared that if any parish priest or any other priest, whether regular or secular, should attempt to unite in marriage or bless the betrothed of another parish, he would, even though he pleaded that his action was based on a privilege or immemorial custom, remain *ipso iure* suspended until he was absolved by the ordinary of that pastor who should have

---

[5] Cf. *supra,* Chapter II, footnote n. 76.

[6] Sess. XXIII, *de ref.,* c. 15.

[7] Sess. XIII, *de ref.,* c. 9; sess. XIV, *de ref.,* c. 8.

been present at the marriage. Moreover, the very validity of the sacrament depended upon the presence of the proper pastor, or of some other priest who assisted at the marriage with that pastor's permission, and of two or three witnesses.[8] This was, indeed, an important factor which helped to clarify the extent of the *cura animarum*.

A blow to the extensive scope of the exclusive rights of the parish church, however, was effected through the Council's instructions regarding attendance at Holy Mass on Sundays and Holy Days. The local ordinaries were merely urged to admonish the faithful to go frequently to their own parochial churches, at least on the greater feast days,[9]—quite a change from the provisions a century before, when a decretalist commented that a parishioner could be physically ejected from a church not his own.[10]

No change was wrought in the status of other parochial functions. These indications of parochial status remained quite the same. It was taken for granted that baptism was ordinarily to be conferred by the pastor of the person to be baptized; but, on the other hand, the privileges accorded the mother and cathedral churches still held. Nothing definite was stated concerning the conferral of the last sacraments or regarding the exclusive rights of the pastor to conduct the burial services. It is certain that these remained reserved parochial functions.

C. *The Church Building; Sufficient Endowment; Permission of the Bishop*

In keeping with the ancient tradition, the Council presupposed the existence of the church building and a sufficient endowment as requirements for the erection of a parish. But the Fathers of the Council decreed that, if the revenues of an already existing parish were insufficient to meet the necessary obligations, then the

---

[8] Sess. XXIV, *de ref.*, c. 1. Although the presence of the *proper* pastor was not mentioned explicitly in this decree, later jurisprudence left no doubt that it was the presence of one's own pastor that was demanded. Cf. Kelly, *The Functions Reserved to Pastors*, p. 35.

[9] Sess. XXII, *Decretum de observandis et evitandis in celebratione Missae.*

[10] Panormitanus, *Commentaria*, Lib. III, tit. 29, cap. II, n. 2.

bishop was to meet the exigency by means of the union of one benefice with another. If the union proved an inadequate solution to the problem, the needs of the rector were to be provided for by the assignment of first-fruits or tithes, by the voluntary contributions of the faithful, or in any other way the bishop might deem advisable.

In taking care that a sufficient means of support was had, the Council enacted a further precaution when it declared that cathedral churches whose revenues did not exceed one thousand ducats annually, and parish churches whose revenues amounted to less than one hundred, were not to be burdened with taxes.[11] Moreover, the privilege of keeping a fourth of the funeral dues (*quarta funeralium*), which many regulars had acquired in the forty years before the Council of Trent, was abrogated in favor of the cathedrals and parishes.[12]

Nothing specific was stated on the permission of the bishop as a requirement for the constitution of a parish, but the inference of its necessity is contained in practically all parochial decrees.[13]

Summary

On the whole the Council of Trent did much to encourage and promote a more orderly parochial system, but the picture of the constitutive elements was little changed by its legislation. An important step forward, however, was the insistence upon a *distinct* group of the faithful as essential in the constitution of a parish. The reserved parochial functions which—though not constitutive elements—served as indications of parochial status were further extended in relation to matrimony, but remained much the same in relation to the other sacraments. Although nothing explicit was stated regarding the church building and the required permission of the bishop in the constitution of a parish, very specific legislation on the endowment and sufficient means of support was enacted.

---

[11] Sess. XXIV, *de ref.*, c. 13.

[12] Sess. XXV, *de ref.*, c. 13.

[13] Sess. XXIII, *de ref.*, c. 15; sess. XXIII, *de ref.*, c. 1; sess. XXIV, *de ref.*, c. 13.

ARTICLE 2. THE CONSTITUTIVE ELEMENTS OF THE PARISH AFTER THE COUNCIL OF TRENT

The period from after the Council of Trent to the time of the enactment of the present Code presented a picture of varying confusion regarding the constitutive elements of the parish. For the first time distinctive lists of constitutive elements were offered, but nowhere did these lists clearly distinguish between what was absolutely essential in the constitution of a parish and what might be termed accessory. This lack of distinction was at the root of all the difficulties. The Roman tribunals and the authors more than once enumerated what was required in the constitution of a parish and gave the impression that they were listing the inherently essential elements.[14] Yet only a slightly further research on the part of the legal historian could unfailingly discover an element that had to be considered as merely accessory.[15]

As one studies the decisions of the Sacred Roman Rota and of the Congregations regarding the parochial status of churches, one's mind seems constantly enmeshed in that type of difficulty. Even a consultation of the authors seemed little able to disperse the welter of confusion. In the maze of contradictory decisions and conflicting opinions, however, a few new developments are discernible. Again for the sake of a more orderly development, the matter will be presented under separate sections in this article.

A. *Territorial Limits*

The existence of territorial limits was mentioned without exception as a constitutive element of the parish by the Rota, by the Sacred Congregations and by the authors.[16] It was intimated in

[14] S. R. Rota, *Tranen.*, 13 ian. 1673—*Decisiones*, 7 pars 18, Tom. I, *recent.*, nn. 1-2, p. 18; *Leodien.*, 20 febr. 1673— *Decisiones*, 32, pars 18, Tom. I, *recent.*, n. 2, p. 62; Pirhing, Lib. III, tit. 29, nn. 1-2; Schmalzgrueber, Lib. III, tit. 29, n. 3; Reiffenstuel, Lib. III, tit. 29, n. 2; Bouix, *Tractatus de Parocho*, p. 173.

[15] Merely to cite one example, cf. S. C. C., *Maceraten.*, 14 mart. 1778—*Thesaurus Resolutionum Sacrae Congregationis Concilii* (167 vols., Romae, 1718-1908), XIII, 49 (hereafter cited *Thes. Resol.*).

[16] See *supra*, footnote n. 14; cf. also Barbosa, *Iuris Ecclesiastici Universi Libri Tres*. Lib. I, cap. XX, n. 18, and Leurenius, *Forum Beneficiale* (2 vols., Venetiis, 1752), Pars I, cap. III, q. 147.

almost every instance that their existence was absolutely essential. Although very often this was true, it definitely was incorrect to include a distinct territory in the generic definition of a parish. For a personal or a family parish was just as much a parish as a parish which was territorially circumscribed. A parish could exist without any territorial boundaries whatsoever.

The actual existence of such parishes both before and after the Council of Trent is an established fact.[17] A consultation of the *Corpus Iuris Canonici* clearly demonstrates that they existed as early as the twelfth century. Special consideration was given at that time to the spiritual care of lepers. In the III General Council of the Lateran (1179), Alexander III (1159-1181) endorsed the establishment of parishes for them, having offered in explanation that they could not be in contact with others apart from some danger of contagion, and that in consequence it was fitting that they have a church of their own.[18]

Innocent III (1198-1216) likewise placed the stamp of approval on personal parishes. The difficulties of language and of rite merited his consideration. When particular groups of the faithful dwelt among those of some other language or rite, special priests were to be assigned to their care.[19] At a somewhat later date special priests were likewise assigned to military encampments for the spiritual welfare of the soldiers.[20]

The existence of personal parishes after the Council of Trent needs no proof. Strangely enough, some of the very authors who included the existence of territorial limits in their generic definition of a parish did not sense any hesitancy in speaking also of parishes "with groups of the faithful distinct not through their residence within distinct territorial limits, but by reason of the different families to which they belonged."[21] Through the eighteenth and

[17] Ciesluk, *National Parishes,* p. 17.

[18] C. 2, X, *de ecclesiis aedificandis vel reparandis,* III, 48.

[19] C. 14, X, *de officio iudicis ordinarii,* I, 31.

[20] De Luca, *Theatrum Veritatis et Iustitiae* (16 vols., Coloniae Aggripinae, 1706), Tom. VIII, disc. XX, n. 19.

[21] Barbosa, *De Officio et Potestate Parochi,* animadversiones et addimenta Ubaldi Giraldi (Romae, 1831) Pars I, cap. I, n. 23 (hereafter cited *De Officio et Potestate Parochi*) ; Leurenius, *Forum Beneficiale,* Pars II, cap. 1, q. 890.

nineteenth centuries the Sacred Congregation of the Council, in seeming contradiction to the Rota's demands for territorial boundaries, again and again maintained the canonical standing of family parishes, and upheld the right of the family pastor to confer the sacraments.[22]

How may one reconcile the actual existence of fully canonical family parishes with the claim that a territorial circumscription is postulated for the existence of a parish? The two factors simply cannot be reconciled. One is forced to state simply that it was an error to include the existence of specified territorial boundaries in the generic idea of a parish. It could be termed nothing more than an accessory element, present indeed in most cases, but not in all.

B. *Group of the Faithful*

As confusing as were the decisions of the Roman Rota and of the Sacred Congregation of the Council with reference to territorial and family parishes, yet it is evident throughout that there was a concerted juridical tendency not to recognize as parochial in character such churches which did not have assigned to them a *distinct* body of the faithful. The parochial status of territorial as well as of family parishes was indeed defended, but both the Rota and the Congregation of the Council, in keeping with the legislation of the Council of Trent,[23] were intolerant of churches which claimed parochial status in the face of the fact that the sacraments were received and administered indiscriminately.[24] A determinate body of the faithful was demanded as an absolutely essential requirement in the constitution of a parish. Whether the group was defined on a territorial or on a family basis was inconsequential,

---

[22] *Spoletana,* 18 iul. 1733—*Thes. Resol.,* VI, 111; *Tolentina,* 11 maii 1748, *Thes. Resol.,* XVII, 43; *Maceraten.,* 14 mart. 1778— *Thes. Resol.,* XLVII, 63; *Sancti Severini,* 25 ian. 1817—*Thes. Resol., LXXVII,* 21.

[23] Sess. XXIV, *de ref.,* c. 13.

[24] Cf. especially S. C. C., *Feltrien.,* 15 iul. 1882—*ASS,* XV (1882), 309. In this decision is quoted a pertinent decree of an Apostolic Visitator, given Aug. 30, 1584; cf. also S. R. Rota, *Leodien.,* 20 febr. 1673—*Decisiones,* 32, pars 18, Tom. I, *recent,* n. 2, p. 62.

although a decided preference was shown towards the specification of the parish group by means of territorial lines or boundaries.

Not much light is to be drawn from the decrees of the Sacred Congregation of the Council regarding the minimum number of people postulated for the erection or continued existence of a parish. When no parishioners were left, it was certain that parochial status was lost.[25] It was certain, too, so the Congregation stated in a decision of December 18, 1762, that one family did not suffice. At least ten were required for the erection of a parish. A lesser number could suffice for the continued maintenance of parochial status, but only if the parish had existed through many years. When only three or four families were left, however, then a cause was given for the uniting of this church with a neighboring parochial church.[26]

With few exceptions, the views of the canonists on the minimum requisite number of parishioners followed the general pattern outlined above. Barbosa (1580-1649) held that a parish could not be constituted with less than ten homes or families, and asserted that the *"mancipia"* in the ancient text (c. 3, C. X, q. 3) which read, *"ecclesia, quae usque ad decem habebit mancipia,"* should have read *"municipia,"* i.e., families or domiciles.[27]

Fagnanus (1598-1678) surprisingly contended that ten persons were sufficient as a material basis for the erection of a parish, and that it was not necessary that all ten had reached the use of reason.[28] Pirhing (1606-1679), however, preferred the view of Barbosa, but added that in his country (Germany) it was the custom to include both Catholic and heretical families in the number.[29]

Reiffenstuel (1642-1703) likewise held that ten families were required, but he reported that it was the practice in his day to ignore

---

[25] *Portuen.*, 19 iul. 1766—*Thes. Resol.*, XXXV, 152.

[26] *Constantien.*—*Thes. Resol.*, XXXI, 279-280.

[27] *De Officio et Potestate Parochi*, Pars I, cap. I, n. 18; Giraldi of St. Cajetan (1692-1775) in his additions to Barbosa's work reported a case in which the Congregation of the Council refused permission to erect a parish when only nine families were had.

[28] *Commentaria in Quinque Libros Decretalium* (4 vols., Venetiis, 1697), Lib. III, tit. 20, n. 28.

[29] *Ius Canonicum in Quinque Libros Decretalium Distributum*, Lib. III, tit. 29, n. 28.

all consideration of the number, and simply to decide whether the parish had a sufficient means of support once it was constituted.[80] The opinion that ten families were required but also sufficed as a basis for the erection of a parish received the approval of Schmalzgrueber (1663-1775). Without any positive sign of approval or of disapproval, he took note of Pirhing's observation that Catholics as well as non-Catholics might be included in the number.[81]

The later commentators adhered to the trend set by the classicists. Ten families were required for the erection of a parish; a lesser number, however, could suffice for the maintenance of a parochial status, especially when the parish had been long established.

C. *The Office of Pastor*

Enumerated as consistently as the existence of territorial limits had been enumerated among the constitutive elements of the parish by the Roman Rota,[82] by the Sacred Congregation of the Council,[83] and also by the authors,[84] was a proper pastor. The office of pastor, as something that could be distinct from the incumbent of the parochial benefice, received no mention. Thus once again there appeared the failure to distinguish between the absolutely essential and accessory elements. Certainly the pastor himself could not be considered absolutely essential. A parish did not cease to be a parish simply because the pastor had become incapacitated, had been transferred, or perhaps had died, and no one else had as yet been appointed in his place. It would have been better, as Mundy lately has stressed, to state that the office of pastor rather than the person himself was to be counted among the inherent requisites for the legally constituted existence of a parish.[85]

The major problem concerning the pastor was of course not one

---

[80] *Ius Canonicum Universum,* Lib. III, tit. 29, n. 7.

[81] *Ius Ecclesiasticum Universum,* Lib. III, tit. 29, n. 7.

[82] *Tranen.,* 13 ian. 1673—*Decisiones,* 7, pars 18, Tom. I, *recent,* n. 1, p. 18.

[83] *Neapolitana,* 29 febr. 1744—*Thes. Resol.,* XIII, 49.

[84] Barbosa, *Iuris Ecclesiastici Universi Libri Tres,* Lib. I, cap. XX, n. 18; Schmalzgrueber, Lib. III, tit. 29, n. 3; Reiffenstuel, Lib. III, tit. 29, n. 2; Leurenius, *Forum Beneficiale,* pars I, cap. III, q. 147.

[85] Cf. *The Union of Parishes,* p. 10.

of terminology. The prime difficulty was in determining the essential elements of the pastoral office. Was a church parochial if the rector had no faculties to baptize? Was it parochial if the right of burial of the members of the rector's flock pertained to a different church? If others gained the right to administer paschal Communion, was parochial status lost? If a restriction was placed on the rector's right of assisting at marriages, did that effect the parochial status? A solution of these problems was of supreme importance.

In theory the administration of all the sacraments was a reserved parochial prerogative,[36] but in the post-Tridentine period many a pastor's rights were restricted in consequence of the cumulative or even exclusive rights claimed by the pastors of cathedral and mother churches. This reservation of rights by superior churches dated as far back as the ninth century,[37] and the practice continued even after the Council of Trent. In a series of cases presented to the Rota and the Sacred Congregation of the Council in the latter part of the seventeenth and throughout the eighteenth and nineteenth centuries, the cathedral and mother churches contended in view of these cumulative and often times exclusive privileges that the filial churches were no more than subsidiary chapels, and accordingly did not merit the title of parish.[38]

One will note in an examination of the cases presented that there was an absence of conflict concerning the question of confession to the pastors, as decreed by the Council of Trent.[39] This was so, for after the middle of the seventeenth century the administration of the sacrament of penance was no longer deemed an exclusive parochial prerogative. It is true that the Council of Trent

---

[36] Conc. Trident., sess. XXIV, *de ref.*, c. 13.

[37] Confer p. 26 of this study.

p. 62; *Leodien.*, 1 dec. 1673—*Decisiones*, 192, pars 18, Tom. I, *recent.*, p. 356; S. C. C., *Boianen.*, 10 maii 1732—*Thes. Resol.*, V, 319; *Neapolitana*, 20 febr. 1744—*Thes. Resol.*, XIII, 49; *Toletana*, 11 maii 1748—*Thes. Resol.*, XVII, 43; *Venusina*, 25 iun. 1763—*Thes. Resol.*, XXXII, 138; *Squillacen.*, 11 dec. 1897—*Thes. Resol.*, CLVI, 1086; *Sypontina*, 12 iun. 1884—*ASS*, XVII (1884), 280.

[38] S. R. Rota, *Tranen.*, 13 ian. 1673—*Decisiones*, 7 pars 18, Tom. I, *recent.*,

[39] Sess. XXIII, *de ref.*, c. 15.

had reserved the administration of the sacrament to the pastor, but it had also declared that for the hearing of confessions the ordinary could approve regulars or seculars, who were in no way obliged to secure the permission of the pastor.[40]

In practice this special concession was extended during the following years even to the paschal confession. When the inevitably resultant dispute between pastors and regulars reached a high pitch, Innocent X (1644-1655) in 1645 specifically decreed that regulars, when approved by the local ordinaries, could not be forbidden to hear the confessions of the faithful during the paschal season. He added, however, that the administration of paschal Communion was forbidden to them.[41] The dispute failed to subside, and Clement X (1670-1676) in 1670 insisted again that the precept of annual confession was fulfilled through submission of one's sins to any approved religious.[42] Thereafter no serious conflict was raised, and hence the question found no place in the cases presented to the Roman Congregations.

The majority of the presented cases concerned the status of churches which lacked baptismal fonts—churches for which there was not acknowledged the right of conferring solemn baptism inasmuch as the right was reserved to cathedral or mother churches.[43] The Congregation of the Council took cognizance of the reservations, but at the same time consistently decreed the parochial status of the filial churches whenever they could produce evidence that a determinate group of people had been assigned to them as under the pastoral care of a specially designated and appointed rector.

Usually the assignment of the parishioners to a particular church was postulated on the principle of territoriality, but in a case presented on May 10, 1732, no such demand was in evidence. Besides the parish church of St. Mary Major in the city of Campo-

---

[40] *Loc. cit.*

[41] Const. *Exponi vobis,* 7 febr. 1645—*Bull. Rom.,* XV, 362.

[42] Const. *Superna,* 21 iun.—*Bull. Rom.,* XVIII, 55.

[43] S. C. C., *Venusina,* 25 iun. 1763—*Thes. Resol.,* XXXII, 138; *Neapolitana,* 29 febr. 1744—*Thes. Resol.,* XIII, 49; *Boianen.,* 10 maii 1732—*Thes. Resol.,* V, 319; *Fabrianen.,* 24 maii 1732—*Codicis Iuris Canonici Fontes,* cura Emi Petri Card. Gasparri editi (9 vols., Romae [postea Civitate Vaticana]: Typis Polyglottis Vaticanis 1923-1939. Vols. VII, VIII, IX, ed. cura et studio Emi Iustiniani Card. Serédi), n. 3292 (hereafter cited *Fontes*).

bosso, Italy, there were three other churches, each of which had its proper rector who exercised the care of souls, the churches being distinct not through any determination of separate territorial limits, but through a differentiation of the families assigned to each of the churches. The baptismal font for the three was, however, reserved to St. Mary Major, which contended on that ground that the other churches were no more than subsidiary chapels. In a response, delayed until May 25 of the same year, the Sacred Congregation denied the contention of St. Mary Major, and pronounced the parochial status of the three churches.[44]

In these and other presented cases the Roman Tribunals and Congregations emphasized the fact that reservations to cathedral and mother churches, and also privileges granted by indult to others or obtained by them through custom or prescription, did not necessarily preclude the existence of parochial status on the part of churches. As early as 1673 the Roman Rota made clear that the absence of the right of granting Christian burial did not prove the non-parochial status of a church, since in the act of dismemberment the mother church was able to reserve that right to itself. Moreover, custom likewise could furnish the basis for the possession of such a right.[45]

The administration of paschal Communion was one of the most closely guarded parochial functions down through the centuries,[46] and yet the Congregation of the Council on June 25, 1763, declared a certain church to be parochial in character, even though the pastor had no right to distribute Easter Communion. By reason of the privilege accorded to the mother church, his flock was obliged to receive there.[47] And so in like cases, one after the other, the parochial status of churches was declared.[48]

---

[44] S. C. C., *Boianen.*, 10 et 25 maii 1732—*Thes. Resol.*, V, 319.

[45] *Tranen.*, 13 ian.—*Decisiones*, 7 pars 18, Tom. I, *recent.*, n. 2, p. 11.

[46] It was only on November 28, 1912, that Pope Pius X decreed that the precept of paschal Communion could be fulfilled in any church, even in those of regulars.—S. C. C., *Decretum—Acta Apostolicae Sedis, Commentarium Officiale* (Romae, 1909—), IV (1912), 726 (hereafter cited *AAS*).

[47] *Venusina—Thes. Resol.*, XXXII, 138.

[48] For a list of cases, cf. Pallottini, *Collectio Omnium Conclusionum et resolutionum quae in causis propositis apud Sacram Congregationem Cardinalium S. Concilii Tridentini Interpretum prodierunt ab eius institutione*

But from all this it is not warranted to conclude that the functions of the rector merited little consideration in the act of determining the status of his church. In a decision of 1825 the Sacred Congregation of the Council declared that the parochial status of a church could not be doubted if baptism was conferred and paschal Communion received there; if Maundy Thursday ceremonies were celebrated; and especially if the Holy Oils were reserved, marriages contracted and funeral services conducted there.[49]

However, if these rights were gained only through apostolic privilege, then, in accord with an earlier decree one must note, these ministrations did not in and of themselves suffice to reveal a parochial character for the church.[50]

The foregoing presentation hardly serves to clarify the issue through any specific identification of the factors and elements inherent in the office of pastor. Exactly what minimum was required if the rector of a church was to be considered as the incumbent of a parish church still remained only vaguely determined at the best.[51] But one may well point out several acknowledged factors as lending aid in certifying the existence of parochial status. In doubt concerning the parochial status of a church, the following indications were to be considered:

1) whether it had a baptismal font;
2) whether the pastor had the right to assist at marriages;
3) whether the right of granting Christian burial was reserved to the church;
4) whether the Holy Oils were reserved there; and
5) whether the rector had the exclusive right of administering paschal Communion.[52]

---

anno MDLXIV ad annum MDCCCLX, distinctis titulis alphabetico ordine per materias digesta (18 vols., Romae, 1868-1895), IX, s.v. *Ecclesia Parochialis,* V (hereafter cited Pallottini).

[49] *Reatina,* 11 iun.—*Thes. Resol.,* LXXXV, 121.

[50] S. C. C., *Constantien.,* 18 dec. 1762—*Thes. Resol.,* XXXI, 277.

[51] Schmalzgrueber (Lib. III, tit. 29, n. 5) contended that under particular circumstances (*ex accidenti*) it was possible for a parish church to exist even when its rector was not authorized for the administration of any of the sacraments other than the sacraments of penance and of the Holy Eucharist.

[52] This last particular point was applicable until 1912, but not thereafter.

If all these signs were present, then, unless they were gained by privilege or through special concession, the church was certainly of a parochial character. If one or the other of these signs was lacking, even then the contrary could not be affirmed immediately.

D. *The Church Building*

It has already been pointed out that the possible erection of a parish without a church of its own was only a post-Tridentine development.[53] It is most difficult to propose the exact year in which the first recorded instance of this kind is found. In a decision of January 25, 1895, the Sacred Congregation of the Council had reference to a decree issued by a certain Archbishop Antonio Marcas De Llanes in Spain a century earlier. The archbishop approved the use of one and the same church by two distinct pastors, and added that the practice had a precedent in other dioceses of Spain, Tortosa and Orihuela among them. In its response of 1895 the Congregation not only recommended the procedure when there was a lack of churches, but stated that the words of the Council of Trent in demanding a church for each pastor,[54] were not to be interpreted with absolute literalness—"*quod non de fabrica materiali intelligitur, ita ut in una ecclesia, plures parochi distinctum gregem per turnum regere possint, extante necessitate, uti in causa.*"[55]

The Sacred Congregation for the Propagation of the Faith likewise acknowledged the same practice in territories under its care. In a case presented by the Archbishop of Quebec in 1875 regarding the *missa pro populo,* the Congregation made clear that two distinct parishes could exist even though they used one and the same church.[56]

Of relevant import was a case presented on June 12, 1917, and appealed on February 9, 1918. In this instance it was specifically

[53] Cf. *supra,* Chapter II, Article 2, Section B.

[54] Sess. XXIV, *de ref.,* c. 13.

[55] *Hispalen.—ASS,* XXVII (1895), 10.

[56] *Quebecen.,* 26 febr.—*Collectanea S. Congregationis de Propaganda Fide* (2 vols., Romae, 1907), n. 1436 (hereafter cited *Collectanea*).

stated; *"Paroecia enim in suo esse iuridico—ut dici solet—cum iuribus et officiis plene constituta esse potest quin propriam ecclesiam habeat."*[57]

So it was that an age-old tradition of fifteen centuries was broken through force of necessity. Although the ideal—a proper church for each parish—was still urged by the Roman Congregation,[58] reality was faced and permission to the contrary was granted when circumstances demanded. No longer could a proper church be considered as an essential element for the existence of a parish. The existence of a proper church was thenceforth rather to be regarded as an accessory element.

E. *The Proper Endowment*

Concerning the proper endowment for a church there were many decisions. The interpretation given by the Sacred Congregation of the Council showed a tendency to establish determined sums for certain localities.[59] Allowing for varying circumstances as to the amount required, the Congregation was nevertheless insistent that the endowment be certain and perpetual, since there was question of an established income for the maintenance of a permanent moral person.[60]

Important was a decision which was given on June 27, 1807. In place of a strict endowment, the free offerings of the faithful were admitted as a suitable patrimony when it could be proved that their payment was substantially reliable.[61] A similar case was the one of December 14, 1895. Reversing a previous decision, the Sacred Congregation declared on that date that a bishop could erect a parish in which no proper endowment was possible, provided, however, that it would be constituted within three years,

---

[57] S. C. C., *Consentina—AAS,* X (1918), 289; cf. Tunzi, *Condizione giuridica della parrochia nel diritto canonico e nel diritto ecclesiastico italiano* (Romae: Univ. Gregoriana, 1938), p. 5.

[58] Cf. especially S. C. C., *Feltrien.,* 15 iul. 1882—*ASS,* XV (1882), 309-325.

[59] *Tudertina,* 27 apr. 1822—Pallottini, XIV, s.v. *Parochus,* IV, n. 90.

[60] *Fanen.,* 22 mart. 1760—*Thes. Resol.,* XXIV, 57.

[61] *Sabinen.—Thes. Resol.,* LXXIII, 130.

and on condition, too, that the things which were necessary for divine worship would not be lacking.[62]

The strict endowment, therefore, was no longer an absolutely essential element in the constitution of a parish. Parishes could and did exist without it,[63] but still a sufficient means of support, in whatever form it existed, had always to be present.

F. *Permission of the Bishop*

Among the most closely guarded rights of the bishop through the centuries of the Church's existence was his administrative power with reference to parochial affairs. Not only were pastors subject to his immediate rule, but their churches depended upon him for their very canonical standing. This principle was exhibited in unmistakable terms through three centuries of post-Tridentine decisions.[64]

The claim of any church to parochial standing was invalid unless the permission of the bishop for its erection was juridically proved;[65] not only this, but further required was also the bishop's or his successor's continued approval of this juristic condition.[66]

Apparently in earlier years an oral permission of the bishop sufficed; but in 1897 the Sacred Congregation of the Council stated that above all things a formal document certifying that permission was required.[67] Certainly the permission of the bishop had to be counted among the absolutely essential elements for the constituting of a parish.

---

[62] *Squillacen.—Analecta Ecclesiastica* (Romae, 1893-1911), III (1895), 486-487.

[63] In the United States, churches have long depended for their support on the voluntary contributions of the faithful, and only in a few rare cases on anything like a strict endowment. Cf. Ayrinhac, *Administrative Legislation in the New Code of Canon Law* (New York: Longmans, Green and Co., 1930), pp. 310-311 (hereafter cited *Administrative Legislation*).

[64] S. R. Rota, *Leodien.*, 20 febr. 1673—*Decisiones,* 32, pars 18, Tom. I, *recent.*, n. 5, p. 62; S. C. C., *Portuen.*, 19 iul. 1766—*Thes. Resol.*, XXXV, 152.

[65] S. C. C., *Portuen.*, 19 iul. 1766—*Thes. Resol.*, XXXV, 152.

[66] S. C. C., *litt.*, 18 mart. 1881—*Collectanea,* n. 1548.

[67] *Squillacen.*, 11 dec.—*Thes. Resol.*, CLVI, 1896. Cf. *Analecta Ecclesiastica,* V (1897), 489.

Addenda

In the preceding treatment of the constitutive elements since the time of the Council of Trent one will note only sparse references to the works of the commentators. This should not be surprising, for, as was intimated in the introduction to the present article, little beyond what is found in the decisions of the Roman Tribunals and Congregations was contributed by them. The research student simply finds references in the works of the authors to these decisions and little, if any, comment, and looks in vain for a much desired distinction between the accessory and the absolutely essential elements constitutive of a parish. Both the accessory and the essential elements were simply listed as constitutive elements, and no further explanation was attempted.

Virtual unanimity existed among the classicists[68] as well as among later pre-Code commentators[69] in enumerating the existence of territorial limits, the incumbency of a proper pastor, and the assignment of a distinct group of the faithful among the constitutive elements. All likewise inferred the necessity of the bishop's permission for the erection of a parish, but Reiffenstuel[70] and Schmalzgrueber[71] were most explicit in their statements regarding this latter demand. Although the strict endowment received rare mention, the first-fruits, tithes, and voluntary offerings of the faithful were rather frequently listed as necessary to the parish.[72] Strangely enough, no references were made to the need of a proper church building as a constitutive element, but seemingly only for the reason that parishes without churches of their own were practically non-existent.

The classicists mentioned other requisites for the parochial status

---

[68] Cf. Barbosa, *De Officio Et Potestate Parochi,* Pars. I, cap. I, n. 27; Reiffenstuel, Lib. III, tit. 29, n. 6; Schmalzgrueber, Lib. III, tit. 29, nn. 3-4.

[69] Maupied, *Juris Canonici Universi Compendium* (2 vols., ed. J. P. Migne, Parisiis, 1863), I, 1212-1217; Ferraris, *Prompta Bibliotheca Canonica, Iuridica, Moralis, Theologica, nec non Ascetica, Polemica, Rubricistica, Historica* (8 vols., Romae, 1885-1899), s.v. *Parochia,* nn. 10-15.

[70] *Ius Canonicum Universum,* Lib. III, tit. 29, n. 6.

[71] *Ius Ecclesiasticum Universum,* Lib. III, tit. 29, n. 2.

[72] Pirhing, Lib. III, tit. 29, n. 3; Leurenius, *Forum Beneficiale,* Pars I, cap. III, q. 160.

of a church, such as the permanency and the unity of the pastoral office.[73] In the nineteenth century, however, the note of unity was more universally acknowledged so that it received less frequent mention. And yet Bouix claimed that unity was not required, and he also stated that subjective permanency in the pastoral office could not be considered as a necessary element with reference to a constituted parish.[74]

Throughout the works of all the authors one will note that particular stress was laid on the possession of power in the penitential forum as an element inherent in the very concept of the pastoral office. This followed from the faithful's obligation of receiving the sacraments from their pastor. Certainly, if the pastor had no faculties to forgive sins, no true pastorate could exist.

Only slightly more than this (and it remains irrelevant to the present study) is derivable from a consultation of the authors. Hence there is no point in lengthening the discussion regarding their views. The foregoing summary presents substantially the consensus of the canonical writers, and thus reflects the various elements which before the law of the present Code were deemed constitutive elements for the erection and the continued existence of a parish.

---

[73] Schmalzgrueber, Lib. III, tit. 29, n. 4; Barbosa, *op. cit., loc. cit.;* Reiffenstuel, Lib. III, tit. 29, n. 7.

[74] *Tractatus de Parocho,* pp. 192-197.

PART II

Canonical Commentary

CHAPTER IV

Territorial Limits

Article 1. Territorial Parishes

A. *General Law*

The history of the parochial institute establishes beyond a doubt that, in reference to the parish in general, territorial limits can be considered nothing more than an accessory element.[1] Although the provisions of the Council of Trent[2] in urging a territorial division of the diocese were heeded almost universally, there existed and there continue to exist parishes which have no territorial boundaries whatsoever. Canon 216, § 4, provides for this exception to the general law.

The necessity for territorial organization is not thereby minimized. The Church has always shown a preference for division on a territorial basis, and recognizes it as the most convenient basis of partition. Maroto (1875-1937) stated that the necessity and the convenience of such a partition arise from three sources:[3]

First of all, they derive from the very nature of things, since a homogenious population cannot conveniently be given adequate spiritual services unless they are properly distributed and organized. With comparatively little difficulty the masses of the faithful living within a certain locality can be subdivided into distinct communities with determined territorial boundaries. There by reason of domicile or quasi-domicile they obtain their proper pastor, who rules them according to the prescripts of the law.[4] Moreover, it may be added that through a territorial organization legislation for the *vagi* can conveniently be enacted. They fall under

---

[1] It is a truism to state that they are absolutely essential in the constitution of the territorial parish itself.

[2] Sess. XXIV, *de ref.*, c. 13.

[3] *Institutiones Iuris Canonici,* II, 111.

[4] Canon 94, § 1.

the authority of the pastor of the territory through which they are passing,[5] and hence are subject to the same laws as the true parishioner. *Peregrini,* although not subjects, are also easily provided for.[6]

A second reason advanced by Maroto is that a territorial division is in accord with the mind of Christ. Christ, besides appointing the Supreme Pontiff as the head of the Church, chose subordinate pastors—bishops among whom the spiritual rule was to be divided. This, however, could be most conveniently done through a territorial organization. A further territorial division of the diocese into parishes is based on the same line of reasoning.[7]

A rather weak but third reason proposed by Maroto is that the Church and the faithful as a whole are the mystical Body of Christ. Just as the human body has many members and organs to enhance its beauty, so should the Church likewise reflect reciprocally differentiated elements in its membership.

Regardless of all the reasons proposed, the recognition of a territorial division as the best form of organization is a commonly accepted fact. It is not surprising, therefore, that the present law commands that the territory of every diocese shall be divided into distinct territorial parts. Each portion shall have its own proper church, to which a determinate people shall be assigned. Over this church shall preside a rector, as a proper pastor for the necessary care of souls.[8]

This provision of the Code is not entirely new; it can almost be

---

[5] Canon 99, § 2.

[6] Canons 732, § 2; 881, § 1; 1245, § 1.

[7] Caesar Badii (1884-1938), on the other hand (referring primarily to diocesan limits), elected to term organization on a personal basis as of positive divine law. Christ, so he stated in a somewhat shallow argument, constituted under the Roman Pontiff bishops who, according to their degree of jurisdiction, represent the Pope. Therefore, a personal division may be termed *iuris divini positivi.* But, he continued, a territorial division is *iuris humani.* However, since a territorial partition is demanded by the very nature of things, it may be called *iuris divini naturalis.* It is impossible, he asserted, to rule great concourses of the faithful unless appropriate territorial divisions are made.—*Institutiones Iuris Canonici* (3. ed., 2 vols., Florentiae, 1921), I, 139.

[8] Canon 216, § 1.

termed a mere renewal of the directions of the Council of Trent,[9] although it is couched in stronger terms. Whereas the Fathers of the Council of Trent, with their addition of the clause *"aut utilori modo,"* left some option in the matter of dividing the diocese into territorial parts, the present law simply states absolutely, "The territory of each diocese shall be divided. . . ."

Not only does the law apply to the diocese, but likewise to abbacies and prelacies *nullius.* Canon 215, § 2, decrees that in law abbacies and prelacies *nullius* fall under the term "diocese," unless the contrary appears from the nature of things or from the context of the law. There is nothing in canon 216, § 1, to indicate that either of these exceptive norms is applicable to abbacies or prelacies nullius in the matter here in question. Hence the law definitely applies to them.

B. *Directive Norms for Defining Parochial Boundaries*

The general law in relation to territorial limits, then, cannot be mistaken. Dioceses, prelacies and abbacies *nullius* are simply to be apportioned into territorial segments, and no excusing circumstances are accepted as valid. But what is to be said of particular norms to be followed in the actual application of the general law? Nowhere in the Code are there found any explicit directives, but worthy general norms which may be followed are the prescriptions of canon law regarding canonical causes for the division of parishes.[10]

The Code lists in the first place as a cause for the division of a parish the difficulty of access to the parochial church for a notable number of the parishioners.[11] Natural obstacles such as rivers, strip mines, or railroad rights-of-way would more than likely constitute a justifiable cause for a division through the fixing of new boundaries for the two parishes, the newly created and the previously existing. Distance, likewise, deserves consideration as a

---

[9] Sess. XXIV, *de ref.*, c. 13.

[10] Canon 1427.

[11] Most of the authors hold, in conformity with the earlier law, that there must be a difficulty of approach for at least ten families. This will be discussed in a later article.

factor, especially in consideration of the parochial school.[12] A division of existing parishes must be expected when the parish churches are separated by too great a distance, so that the faithful find attendance at Mass a considerable inconvenience, and find it next to the impossible to send their children to the parochial school.[13]

A second cause for a division as mentioned in Canon 1427, § 2, is "too great a number of the faithful, who cannot be given an adequate spiritual care through provision according to the norms of canon 476, § 1 (through the appointment of additional assistants)." The adequate care of souls should be the prime consideration of the ordinary in drawing parochial boundaries. In congested areas of the larger cities perhaps the territory of the parish should cover no more than several city blocks.

Financial considerations also enter into a determination of parochial boundaries. Never, except in very unusual circumstances,[14] should a territory be so circumscribed that within its limits there is not to be a sufficient number of the faithful for assuring an adequate means of support for the parish. This is to be kept in mind, especially if it means that the new parish will contain territory where there dwell people who would not find it difficult to approach their former parish church. Certainly, for such financial considerations the ordinary is justified in setting the boundaries of the new parish very close to the former parish church. On the other hand, of course, he must not fix the limits in such manner that the older parish would suffer an unreasonable financial loss. A sufficient means of support for the mother church must always remain.[15]

Finally, the ordinary is to keep in mind a declaration of the Sacred Congregation of the Consistory of August 1, 1919: "If

---

[12] Distance from the school is not listed as a canonical cause. However, it certainly merits consideration in the fixing of parochial boundaries.

[13] The Council of Tribur (895) considered a distance of four miles as the utmost distance that should separate one parish church from another (Canon 14—Mansi, XVIII A, 140), but certainly that standard is hardly applicable in modern times.

[14] Canon 1415, § 3.

[15] Canon 1427, § 3.

the scanty or fluctuating population, or the absolute want of an endowment (*dos*) make it far from advisable to erect certain churches into parishes, let these churches be considered as subsidiary churches or chaplaincies within the boundaries of some parish upon which they shall remain dependent, until they can become parishes themselves."[16]

Since interference with determined parochial limits always involves either the division or the dismemberment of a benefice, for the execution of which canonical causes are needed, the boundaries must be fixed with permanence. No temporary arrangements are permissible. Hence the markers by which the limits are designated should not be destructible, transitory or movable objects such as buildings, residences, parks, golf courses, farms—anything that is subject to change by private authority.[17] Nor should the boundaries be such that their identification is subject to change through an act of intervention by the civil authority.[18] Such would be the designation of parochial boundaries with the term "city limits." State limits or county lines, however, seem to offer an adequate degree of permanency.

Safe markers for defining boundaries are generally any permanent natural landmarks such as rivers, mountains and valleys. Sectional lines, city streets, highways, railroad rights-of-way also serve the purpose very well. However, it is to be noted that the limits are not to be identified with the markers by which they were defined if these markers have undergone some change. If through some unforeseen circumstance the marker suffers some change, e.g., through a sudden shifting of the course of a stream, or through the re-routing of a railroad right-of-way or of a city street, the actual parochial boundaries remain the same. Nevertheless a determination of the exact parish limits may thereby be rendered difficult.

---

[16] *AAS,* XI (1919), 346.

[17] Cf. Chelodi, *Ius de Personis* (3. ed., cura P. Ciprotti, Vicenza: Societa Anonima Tipografica, 1942), p. 344, footnote n. 1.

[18] Caesar Badii (*Institutiones Iuris Canonici,* I, 140, footnote n. 1) disproves the right of any state to interfere with ecclesiastical boundaries. He does admit, though, that the state can request that such boundaries conform to the territorial limits of the country, especially if non-conformity would give rise to difficulties with an inimical state.

Virtual unanimity exists among the authors in their insistence upon a second characteristic in the territorial limits, i.e., that they be distinct and certain. A precise description of the boundaries must be found in every case.[19] This is confirmed in various Rotal decisions.[20] Yet some authors seem willing to abstract from this characteristic. Beste in his commentary on a papal rescript to the Apostolic Delegate of the United States, issued November 10, 1922,[21] states the following:

> Neque necesse est, nostra sententia, ut fines accurate describantur in unoquoque casu erectionis, sed sufficit, ut habeatur regula generalis omnibus casibus aeque applicabilis, vi cuius v.g. linea, quae medium locum occupat inter duas paroecias finitimas, vulgo halfway line, constituat limites inter utramque paroeciam exsistentes cum iis accidentalibus modificationibus quas ordinarius prudenti suo arbitrio in concerto addicere statuat in actu erectionis.[22]

Bernier is of a somewhat similar though less drastic opinion. He declares that the Instruction of the Sacred Congregation for the Propagation of the Faith with regard to the setting of limits for quasi-parishes may be applied also relative to parishes dependent upon the Sacred Congregation of the Consistory. The aforesaid decision orders that the erection of a quasi-parish is to be done by means of a decree of the ordinary, which shall clearly define the boundaries of the territory, or, if this is impossible, shall at least state the principal Christian settlements belonging to it.[23] Bernier

---

[19] Barbosa, *De Officio et Potestate Parochi,* Pars I, cap. I, n. 27; Pirhing, Lib. III, tit. 29, n. 1; Leurenius, *Forum Beneficiale,* Pars I, cap. III, qu. 160; Schmalzgrueber, Lib. III, tit. 29, n. 3; Rossi, *De Paroecia,* p. 21.

[20] S. R. Rota, *Bononien.,* 21 iul. 1911—*Decisiones,* III (1911), 357, n. 6; S. R. Rota, *Iurisdictionis Parochialis,* 14 maii 1912—*Decisiones,* IV (1912), 230.

[21] Bouscaren, *Canon Law Digest* (2 vols., Vol. I, 1934; Vol. II, 1943, Milwaukee: The Bruce Publishing Co., 1934-1943), I, 149-151 (hereafter cited *Digest*).

[22] *Introductio in Codicem,* p. 226.

[23] *Instructio,* 25 iul. 1920—*AAS,* XII (1920), 331.

argues that where similar circumstances prevail in fully canonical dioceses this Instruction has at least a directive force.[24]

It seems to this writer that Bernier's opinion may be upheld. (After all, the ordinary of the canonical diocese would have no other choice should it be impossible to clearly define parochial boundaries in a given case.) Yet Beste's statement seems to be too sweeping. The ordinary cannot, as a general rule, simply decree that the halfway line constitutes the parochial limits between two churches. The description is too inadequate and could give rise to many difficulties involving the rightful use of jurisdiction and the properly authorized administration of the Sacraments.

C. *Prescription and Territorial Limits*

To forestall annoying bickerings and endless controversies, the Church early in its history found it necessary to declare the limits of parishes non-prescriptible, when these had once been defined and fixed with certainty.[25] A renewal of the decree in the present Code of Canon Law causes no surprise.[26]

It is to be noted, however, that the boundaries must be certain before the possibility of legal prescription is precluded. This was emphatically stressed in a number of cases brought before the various Roman tribunals.[27] An interesting case is one that was tried before the Sacred Roman Rota on February 5, 1918. It illustrates clearly the necessity of an accurate description of the parochial boundaries. In view of its practicality (a like dispute could possibly arise in this country) and in view of its informative character regarding the mode of procedure in such cases, it seems warranted to report the case in a rather thorough fashion.

---

[24] *De Patrimonio Paroeciali* (Quebeci, apud Auctorem, 2, via Port Dauphin, 1938), p. 48.

[25] C. 4, X, *de parochiis et alienis parochianis,* III, 29; cf. p. 21 of this dissertation.

[26] Canon 1509, 4°.

[27] S. C. Consist., *Neapolitana et Putertana,* 22 aprilis 1882— *Thes. Resol.,* CXLI (1882), 190; S. R. Rota, *Derthonen.* (Finium Parochialium seu Domorum Vindicationis), 3; ian. 1919 coram R. P. D. Gulielmo Sebastianelli, Decano—*AAS,* XI (1919), 470; S. R. Rota, *Iurisdictionis Parochialis,* 14 maii 1912, coram R. P. D. Antonio Perathaner—*Decisiones,* IV (1912), 230.

At one time there existed in the diocese of Geneva, Switzerland, a monastery to whose parochial care was entrusted the community at Viuz (later called Viuz-Faverges). A neighboring chapel existed at Faverges. By virtue of a papal bull (that of Leo X), the parochial church at Viuz together with the chapel at Faverges were united to the cathedral chapter at Annecy, to which town the episcopal see had been transferred. A rector was then installed at Faverges, who exercised the *cura animarum* both at Faverges and at Viuz-Faverges. With an increase in population, two permanent vicarages, independent of each other, were established in 1763. The incumbents of the vicarages had charge of distinct parts of the parish, the title regarding the care of souls remaining vested with the Chapter at Annecy. Affairs remained such for forty years until the Napoleonic Concordat, when every parish in France was suppressed, so that in consequence thereof the bishop had to petition the consent of the government before new territorial limits of parishes could be drawn. In 1803 the Most Reverend Rene de Merinville, Bishop of Annecy, erected two completely independent and true parishes in the localities of Faverges and Viuz-Faverges.

There was no discord concerning the established parochial limits until the end of the nineteenth century, when a railroad was constructed from the town of Annecy to the town of Albertville. The railroad right-of-way passed through the open territory between the two parishes. At a middle point a new station called Faverges was erected. A number of other buildings and residences also arose in the surrounding locality. Both pastors claimed the new inhabitants as their parishioners.

To settle the dispute the bishop decreed in 1899 that the territory between the middle gate of the Faverges cemetery and the railroad right-of-way *pro tempore* belonged to the parish of Viuz-Faverges. In 1900 his successor initiated a formal action to establish the territory as belonging to Faverges. The ordinary, since the territorial limits seemed so uncertain, claimed his right under the Council of Trent (sess. XXIV, *de ref.*, c. 13) to establish determinate boundaries. A greater portion of territory was granted to the parish of Faverges. The pastor at Viuz-Faverges objected to the bishop's decision, claiming that he thereby lost too great a portion of his parish. He appealed to the Sacred Congregation of the Council. Since the Congregation deemed the case not administrative but judicial in character, it referred the appeal to the diocesan tribunal. The bishop then modified his decision on the territorial limits, but the pastor of Viuz-Faverges was still dissatisfied and brought his case to the Sacred Roman Rota.

The Rota first decided that the burden of proof fell on the pastor at Viuz-Faverges, since his recourse was only *"contra decretum episcopi (pro quo stat praesumptio iuris)."* The ordinary had simply used his right to establish determinate parochial limits where he thought none had existed. The pastor at Faverges, the Rota asserted, was simply seeking to sustain the decree of the ordinary both in the first instance and in the tribunal of appeal. Therefore it was necessary that the pastor of Viuz-Faverges establish that grave injury was wrought to him through the decree of the ordinary which took away territory that was his, since it had been circumscribed by definite and certain limits.

The pastor at Viuz-Faverges failed to do this. It was shown that certain and determinate limits were not made—at least that the presumption was such. The Rota added that, in the hypothesis that lineal divisions were established, no change could be made, except in accordance with the norms and solemnities of the law, since the limits of a parish, once they are certainly fixed, are no longer amenable to legal prescription.

The Rota therefore upheld the decree of the ordinary, and stated that the two parishes were to share the judicial expenses.[28]

In consequence it is stressed once again that the boundaries must be accurately and certainly determined before the possibility of legal prescription is precluded. If perchance the bishop in erecting particular parishes has failed to determine the limits accurately, he can, as long as the effect of legal prescription has not set in, claim his right under the Council of Trent and under Canon 216, § 1, to accomplish this without the formalities of any judicial procedure. If, on the other hand, prescription has taken place (possession in good faith over a period of thirty years),[29] the ordinary must recognize the boundaries as so determined and cannot by means

---

[28] S. R. Rota, *Annecien.*, Finium Parochialium 5 febr. 1918, coram R. P. D. Ioanne Prior—*AAS*, XI (1919), 146-153.

[29] Canon 1511, § 2.

of a simple decree change them. A change under such circumstances involves a dismemberment, which entails a number of legal requirements. An authentic document must be drawn up, signed and sealed; a meeting of the diocesan consultors must be convoked for the purpose of discussing the change; interested parties must be heard.[30]

ARTICLE 2. QUASI-PARISHES

The distinction between parishes and quasi- parishes must not be so unduly urged that it will be thought that a quasi-parish shares only by way of participation or similitude in the nature of a strictly so called parish. On the contrary, it is to be emphasized that a quasi-parish contains all the elements of a properly so called parish, for the Code itself places quasi-pastors on an equal basis with pastors in relation to all the parochial rights and obligations, and, moreover, declares them as coming under the name of pastor in the law.[31]

So much do the parish and the quasi-parish, and the pastor and the quasi-pastor, share the same legal nature that, when an apostolic prefecture or vicariate is constituted as a diocese, its quasi-parishes and quasi-pastors automatically become strict parishes and pastors. A reversal of that procedure, likewise automatic in its juridical effect, is exemplified in the conversion of the parish and the pastor to the status of a quasi-parish and a quasi-pastor.[32] And yet, needless to say, there are accidental differences between the two. As has been stated, the essential note of distinction is founded on the hierarchical unit of which they form a part. Moreover, the incumbents differ in relation to the stability of their office,[33] in relation to their appointment to the office,[34] and in relation to the obligatory application of the *missa pro populo*.[35]

But the most important question at this point is: Do the parish and the quasi-parish differ in relation to territorial limits? Here,

[30] Canon 1428.

[31] Canon 451, § 2, 1°.

[32] Maroto, *Institutiones Iuris Canonici,* II, 140.

[33] Canon 454, § 4.

[34] Canon 457.

[35] Canon 466, § 1.

too, there exist accidental differences. The same general obligation of dividing his territory applies to the vicar and prefect apostolic as it applies to the bishop, but the vicariate and prefecture apostolic is to be divided only "when it can conveniently be done."[36] No such qualifying clause applies to the division of the diocese; no excusing circumstances are admitted in the law. The reason for the distinction becomes immediately apparent. The vicariate and prefecture apostolic are branches of the Church in the process of development; they bespeak an embryonic organization. Unsurveyed territory, a scattered Christian population, lack of funds and a scarcity of priests are characteristic of most of them. The ordinary, in circumstances such as these, is not called on to do more than he can, and so it is not surprising that he is given some option relative to the very consideration of dividing the territory at all.

These same primitive conditions, as they are found in vicariates and prefectures apostolic, often exist in territories, which, although they have a hierarchical organization, are still under the Sacred Congregation for the Propagation of the Faith. Such was the condition in the United States not much more than one hundred years ago. When the first bishops of this country appointed priests, they commissioned them with a more or less general care of the faithful in a rather indefinite territory.[37] This was done only under the stress of the existing circumstances.

When conditions warranted a change, the II Plenary Council of Baltimore (1866) prescribed that, since it was contrary to the laws and customs of the Church and to the efficient care of souls to have many priests in one locality exercising the care of souls independently of one another, and since such a practice all too readily begot confusion, the bishops place one pastor over each and every set parochial territory.[38] The Council further provided

---

[36] Canon 216, § 2.

[37] Golden, *Parochial Benefices in the New Code,* The Catholic University of American Canon Law Studies, n. 10 (Washington, D. C.: The Catholic University of America, 1925), p. 98 (hereafter cited *Parochial Benefices*).

[38] *Concilii Plenarii Baltimorensis II Acta et Decreta* (Baltimorae: Joannes Murphy et Soc., 1868), Tit. III, Cap. IV, n. 111 (hereafter cited *Acta et Decreta II*).

(without making it strictly obligatory) that throughout all the provinces, and especially in the larger cities where there were many churches, districts with accurately fixed limits be assigned to each parish.[39] This latter provision was renewed by the III Plenary Council of Baltimore (1884).[40]

In 1920 the ordinaries of such dioceses which were still under the jurisdiction of the Sacred Congregation for the Propagation of the Faith, evidently finding the same difficulties as existed in the early history of this country, proposed several questions to the Sacred Congregation. Among other things, since their territories were dioceses and not vicariates or prefectures apostolic, they questioned whether they were obliged by the prescription of Canon 216, § 1. Accordingly the Congregation provided:

> 1. As the dioceses subject to this Sacred Congregation are to be considered as missions, some parts of the territory may be permitted to remain undivided, that is, without any designation of parish limits.
>
> 2. But those parts of the territory which have already been assigned definite boundaries, or which hereafter will be assigned such boundaries in accordance with Canon 216, are to be called parishes. They shall, however, be subject to the peculiar provisions that have been made for quasi-parishes.[41]

Although the prescription of the Code (Canon 216, § 2) in relation to vicariates and prefectures apostolic seems very clear by way of comparison with the law for the aforementioned dioceses, still there was occasion for many doubts. These doubts necessitated an Instruction from the Sacred Congregation for the Propagation of

[39] Volumus igitur ut per omnes hasce provincias, praesertim majoribus in urbibus ubi plures sunt ecclesiae, districtus quidam, paroeciae instar, descriptis accurate limitibus, unicuique ecclesiae assignetur; ejusque rectori jura parochialia vel quasi-parochialia tribuantur.—*Acta et Decreta II,* Tit. III, Cap. IV, n. 124.

[40] *Acta et Decreta Concilii Plenarii Baltimorensis Tertii, A. D. MDCCCLXXXIV* (Baltimorae: John Murphy, 1886), Tit. II, Cap. V, n. 32.

[41] *Decretum,* 9 dec. 1920—*AAS,* XIII (1921), 17; cf. Bouscaren, *Digest,* I, 149.

the Faith on July 25, 1920. The territory of all vicariates and prefectures apostolic, so the Instruction began, were to be divided into distinct parts, each having its own population, its own church and its own pastor according to canon 216, § 2. But the ordinaries of such territories were reminded that, while such a division was to be prepared for, and as soon as possible made, yet it was not to be made prematurely. Financial considerations were to be taken into account, and above all the prime consideration was the good of souls through a suitably adapted propagation of the Catholic Faith.

The vicars and prefects apostolic were further advised that it was neither necessary nor desirable to wait until the entire territory could be divided. Quasi-parishes were to be erected whenever sufficiently favorable conditions warranted their erection. If a clear definition of the boundaries of the territory was impossible, then there were to be designated at least the principal Christian communities that were to form the quasi-parish, as also the principal church and the residence of the quasi-pastor.[42]

This Instruction was rather complete, so that little more needs to be added concerning the question of the territorial limits of quasi-parishes. Notice, however, should be taken of the fact that the territorial limits of quasi-parishes are not explicitly listed in canon 1509, 4°, as a matter with reference to which the agency of legal prescription cannot become applicable. Since canon 1509 contains exceptions to the ordinary import of the law, it is subject to a strict interpretation.[43] It could seem, therefore, that the ruling of this canon is not to be regarded as applicable with reference to the established boundaries of a quasi-parish. However, since the quasi-parish and the parish are of the same legal nature and differ only in accidentals, one may rather argue that there is no need of such an explicit mention, since in listing the certainly established and fixed parish boundaries as not subject to change through the agency of legal prescription canon 1509, 4°, implicitly makes its exceptive ruling applicable also to similarly established boundaries of quasi-parishes.

---

[42] *AAS*, XII (1920), 331.
[43] Canon 19.

ARTICLE 3. NATIONAL OR MIXED PARISHES

Canon 216, § 1, clearly implies that in each territorial division of a diocese there is to be but one church, presided over by one pastor, who exercises exclusive jurisdiction over the *general* population of the district. Since the Council of Trent[44] this has been the constant law of the Church, its purpose being, on the one hand, the avoidance of the indiscriminate administration and reception of the Sacraments, and, on the other hand, the fostering of a closer relationship between pastor and people. But ecclesiastical laws must at times yield to the force of circumstance. If strict adherence to a law brings about harm rather than good, an exception to the law must be admitted.

This state of affairs obtained with the influx of millions of immigrants to this country. Inasmuch as their spiritual needs could not be adequately satisfied through the ministrations of an English-speaking pastor, the erection of new churches presided over by a pastor of their own tongue was necessitated. Over these people of foreign tongue the national pastor exercises the same jurisdiction as other pastors. While in some cases his jurisdiction is strictly personal and can be exercised in any part of the world over his subjects,[45] in most instances it is territorially limited.

At times the boundaries are well defined—thus, e.g., in many of our cities where there are found large groups of the faithful of the same nationality. In such places there often is need for more than one national parish for the faithful of the same nationality. In keeping the spirit of the Council of Trent, strict parochial boundaries are then assigned to each church with a view to fostering a close relationship between the pastor and his people.

At other times, although it is not outlined by means of clear and distinct boundaries, the national parish, with the approbation of the ordinary, is assigned a certain general district. This may be an entire city or county with the surrounding areas. But it is difficult to conceive that with exclusive reference to a given group of

---

[44] Sess. XXIV, *de ref.*, c. 13.

[45] Studies and Conferences, "National Pastors and Assistance at Marriage," *The Ecclesiastical Review* (Philadelphia, 1889-1943; Baltimore, 1944— LXXX (1929), 89 (hereafter cited *ER*).

nationals an entire diocese would be placed under the care of one national pastor, in view namely of the practical impossibility of a mutual co-operation between the pastor and the faithful.[46] Yet, in an exceedingly small diocese this desired mutual co-operation could still remain achievable. In that instance there would be no parochial boundaries other than that of the diocese itself. Their limits would be identical, so that the national pastor could exercise his jurisdiction in any part of the diocese.[47]

Various objections have been raised to the view that most of the national parishes in our country possess territory cumulatively with territorial parishes. The manifest intention of the law, it is stated, is to grant exclusive jurisdiction over a certain territory to one pastor. While this statement is partially true, it is not exact and precise. The intention of the law is rather to grant exclusive jurisdiction over a certain territory for the *general* population of the district.[48]

It is true that, should a national parish exist within the boundaries of the territorial parish, the national pastor cannot claim jurisdiction over the general population residing there. His church cannot be one which is *primarily* territorial in character. Domicile and quasi-domicile cannot be employed as *primary* bases for determining membership in the national parish. Therefore a further determinant factor must be sought, and it is found in the diversity of language or in the diversity of nationality which will exist between the general population and those destined to belong to the national parish. The exclusive jurisdiction of the territorial pastor over the general population is thus preserved, while a foundation is provided for the cumulative jurisdiction of the national pastor.

Another objection offered to the presence of a national pastor in the territory of an English-speaking parish is that a conflict of jurisdictional rights is unavoidable. Diversity in language could serve as a determining factor for membership in the one or the other of the two parishes for a time, but what is to be done when

[46] Ciesluk, *National Parishes,* p. 50.

[47] Mundy, *The Union of Parishes,* p. 10.

[48] Bastnagel, "Is a Parish for Colored People a 'National' Parish." *ER,* CVIII (1943), 384.

the parishioners of the national parish have learned English and no longer labor under the language difficulty? As long ago as 1897 that possible clash of rights was anticipated, and the Sacred Congregation for the Propagation of the Faith, to which this country was then still subject, issued an Instruction that was to serve as a guide for the future. The Instruction follows: 1. "Children born in America of non-American parents who speak a language other than English are not bound, when they are emancipated, to join the quasi-parish in which the language of the country (or English) is used." 2. "Catholics who were not born in America but who know the English language have the right to become members of that church in which the English language is in use, and they are not to be obliged to subject themselves to the jurisdiction of the rector of the church which was established for people speaking the language of their own nation."[49]

Hence, it does not rest with the pastor of either the territorial or the national parish to decide to whom his jurisdiction will extend. The foreign-born Catholics or their progeny alone are to choose whether they will join the English-speaking parish or remain members of the national parish. Of course, upon that depends the pastor's jurisdiction. It is to be noted that by occasionally attending services at the territorial church, a person does not necessarily indicate his intention of joining the parish. That intention he may express by enrolling his name in the parish records, by accepting "contribution envelopes" from the church, or by means of his frequent reception of the sacraments and regular attendance at parochial functions.[50]

Difficulties, however, are not so easily overcome when one who by law belongs to the territorial parish desires to affiliate with a national parish. The case is not a rare one, for it frequently happens that the pastor of the national church employs the foreign idiom only on occasions, so that rather generally he conducts the parochial functions in the English language. Moreover, by reason of its proximity the national church is oftentimes easier of access to a portion of the faithful who by reason of domicile or quasi-

---

[49] 26 apr. 1897—*ASS*, XXX (1897), 256. The translation is furnished by the present writer.

[50] Ciesluk, *National Parishes*, p. 107.

domicile belong to the territorial parish. Must they forego the convenience of personally benefiting from the ministration of the strictly parochial functions at the nearby church, where they can easily be accommodated?

The tenor of the law indicates that they must. Canon 216, § 1, in the light of all the earlier pertinent legislation establishes the fact that the Church favors partition on a territorial basis. One pastor should exercise jurisdiction over all the faithful who reside within certain limits. It is stressed again that only by reason of necessity and expediency have there been established national parishes, with language as the primary determinant factor for membership and territory as the secondary. The establishment of such parishes is a divergence from ecclesiastical preference. Their abnormal condition is clearly shown by canon 216, § 4, which requires an apostolic indult for their erection. To belong to such parishes is a privilege accorded to a limited number of faithful who are of a particular nationality; to belong to the territorial parish is a right and a duty for the general populace.[51] Therefore, it is certainly contrary to the law to admit one who cannot claim language or nationality as a determinant factor to membership in a national parish.

But still one could object that the legislator did not foresee the present particular circumstances which exist in this country. Certainly it would not be his mind to impose hardships upon the faithful, and to expect them to retain membership in a territorial parish miles away from their residence when language barriers prove no obstacle to their membership in a nearby national church, which serves just as well and perhaps even better than the territorial parish. The objection beyond doubt has its merits; nevertheless the law stands. It should be remarked, however, that the faithful cannot be obliged under pain of sin to attend services in their own territorial church, and certainly the national pastor who may be accomplishing much spiritual good by allowing non-members to take part in the services furnished at his church does nothing that trespasses against the rights of the territorial pastor.

---

[51] Studies and Conferences, "National and Canonical Parishes in the United States," *ER,* LXXVI (1927), 90-91.

The only practical solution for the problem consists in one of two procedures.

1. The ordinary may seek to obtain a change of the status of the national parish into one of a territorial nature. This would presuppose the fixing of clear parochial boundaries as a condition for the conferral of jurisdiction over the general population to the newly created territorial pastor. Such action would, of course, necessitate an apostolic indult, for, once a national parish is erected, *"nihil innovandum, inconsulta Apostolica Sede."*[62] Moreover, since such an action involves a dismemberment for one or more territorial parishes, the formalities of Canon 1427 would likewise have to be observed.

2. While allowing the national parish to retain its original status in relation to those who are of a particular nationality, the ordinary may nevertheless assign territorial boundaries to the parish in which the pastor may exercise jurisdiction over the general populace. The parish thereby acquires a double nature. It becomes both territorial and national, the determinants for membership being domicile and quasi-domicile for those living within certain limits, and language for a number who live outside the boundaries. Since such procedure involves dismemberment, the ordinary formalities of law are postulated and, because it involves a substantial change in the nature of the parish, an apostolic indult is thereby necessitated.

Before the termination of this chapter, a final word on the non-prescriptibility of the territorial limits of national churches is in place. Certainly canon 1509, 4°, applies to such boundaries just as it applies to the limits of territorial parishes, for a national parish is as much a parish in every sense of the word as is the territorial parish. However, it more frequently happens that the territorial boundaries of national churches are not sufficiently determinate to preclude the possible operation of legal prescription. In that instance, custom and the lapse of time may well be the means of setting canonical boundaries. If in view of the previous uncertainty of the boundaries the effect of legal prescription has intervened, then the ordinary must grant due legal recognition to the boundaries that have become determined through the operative agency of legal prescription.

---

[62] Canon 216, § 4.

CHAPTER V

Determinate Group of the Faithful

ARTICLE 1. FURTHER DETERMINING FACTORS FOR MEMBERSHIP IN A PARISH

Absolutely essential among the constitutive elements of a parish is a *determinate* group of the faithful. As much emphasis must be placed on the word "determinate" as on the phrase "group of the faithful." Just as a parish cannot exist without a body of the faithful,[1] so neither can it exist unless that body of the faithful is sufficiently determinate. The famed decree of the Council of Trent[2] established this beyond question, and canon 216, § 1, clearly demonstrates the fact that a determinate group of parishioners is required in the present law.

In the preceding chapter it was shown that the preferred method of assigning a determinate population to a parish consisted in the fixing of territorial limits for the proper identification of this population. National or mixed parishes, such as depended both on territory and on language as determining factors for their membership, were described as exceptions to the law. Exceptional, too, are the purely personal parishes—parishes without any territorial limits whatsoever. Membership in the personal parish can be claimed only by reason of some personal characteristic. These personal qualities are many and varied, but all in themselves can serve as sufficient bases for providing a definite population to a parish.

1. Mentioned first in canon 216, § 4, is the personal factor of language (*sermo*). Since language or national parishes are ordinarily provided with territorial limits as a secondary factor for the determination of their membership, sufficient consideration has been given to them in the preceding chapter.

---

[1] Cf. chap. II, art. 2, sec. B.

[2] Sess. XXIV, *de ref.*, c. 13; cf. p. 58.

2. A second personal quality enumerated in the canon is citizenship in a certain country (*natio*).[3] The present law thus provides for the erection of separate parishes for people who are of the same tongue but who differ in their citizenship. Such parishes are rare; hardly ever is there any real necessity for them. One could indeed imagine circumstances in which the people of a certain tongue would on purely "patriotic" grounds refuse to merge with others of the same tongue in a particular parish in a foreign country. More often, though, it is the consideration of utility that calls for the erection of such separate parishes. As has been stated frequently, the prime concern of the Church is the salvation of souls. Hence, for instance, if it is to the spiritual welfare of all Americans who live in a foreign city or town to belong to a distinct parish, the Church sanctions such an arrangement.

3. A third quality mentioned in canon 216, § 4, is membership in a certain family (*qualitas familiaris*). Usually this type of parish is limited to the nobility.[4] At times the pastor of such personal parishes finds his jurisdiction limited to a certain city or district. Ordinarily, however, his jurisdiction is not restricted within territorial limitations, so that he can exercise it in any part of the world.[5]

4. Included under the classification of personal parishes are the parishes which serve the rulers of state. An apostolic indult for this type of parish is granted, not by reason of any family characteristic, but because of the honor and the respect that are due to those who are in authority. Membership in the parish is open, not only to the members of the family of the ruling authority, but oftentimes also to those who are in any way connected with the family, such as advisers, secretaries, servants, etc.

5. No specific mention of any other type of personal parishes is made in canon 216, § 4, but authors seldom fail in their commentaries on this canon to make reference to military chaplaincies as connoting the existence of personal parishes.[6] Nevertheless, it

---

[3] Maroto, *Institutiones Iuris Canonici*, II, 115; Ciesluk, *National parishes*, p. 61.

[4] Maroto, *op. cit.*, II, 116.

[5] Ferreres, *Institutiones Canonicae* (editio altera, 2 vols., Barcinone, 1920), I, 231-233.

is absolutely certain that military chaplaincies do not in each and every instance point to the existence of personal parishes. Whether the chaplain may be looked upon as a personal pastor depends upon the special arrangements which the Holy See has made in the different countries.[7]

Ferreres (1861-1936) stated definitely that Spanish military chaplains are considered as personal pastors, although their jurisdiction in relation to matrimony is of a somewhat inferior variety than that which is given to pastors of ordinary parishes.[8] In Italy likewise the military chaplains possess a true parochial jurisdiction;[9] nevertheless the obligation of applying the *missa pro populo* does not fall on them.[10]

Military chaplains in France and Belgium are personal pastors, but for their jurisdiction they depend on the local ordinary, and so it is of a somewhat limited character. They must have recourse to each local ordinary as they travel from place to place, since their delegated jurisdiction does not extend beyond the territory of the one conceding it. Nevertheless, when moving on the battlefield they may absolve soldiers even apart from any positive approval of the local ordinary for his tacit consent may then be assumed.[11]

There is no doubt that the chaplains in the United States military service must be looked upon as personal pastors. The norms enacted by the Sacred Consistorial Congregation for the military

[6] Connolly, *The Canonical Erection of Parishes,* p. 11; Cappello, *Summa Iuris Canonici,* I, 440; Chelodi, *Ius de Personis,* p. 344; Ciesluk, *National Parishes,* p. 15; Maroto, *Institutiones Iuris Canonici,* II, 118.

[7] Canon 451, § 3; cf. Connolly, *op. cit.,* p. 11.

[8] *Institutiones Canonicae,* I, 233.

[9] "In Italia, cappellani militares sunt parochi cum iurisdictione personali et locali, non autem territoriali,"—Cocchi, *Commentarium in Codicem Iuris Canonici* (8 vols. in 5, Vol. III, 4. ed. Taurinorum Augustae: Marietti, 1937), III, 391, footnote n. 2.

[10] Cappello, *Tractatus Canonico-moralis de Sacramentis* (3 vols. in 6, Vol. I, 4. ed., Romae: Marietti, 1945), I, 560. Cf. the same author's *Summa Iuris Canonici,* I, 444, footnote n. 4, where he states that by decree of the 22nd of May, 1919, military chaplains in Spain were freed from the obligation of the *missa pro populo.* Therefore, he continues, the same must be said for the chaplains in France, Belgium and Germany.

[11] Claeys Bouuaert-Simenon, *Manuale Juris Canonici* (3 vols., Vols. I et III, 4. ed., Gandae et Leodii: Dessain, 1934), I, 309.

ordinariate demonstrate this quite clearly. According to the faculties issued on July 1, 1940, the essential elements are present. A determinate group of the faithful is had; the office of chaplain embraces the full parochial powers; a sufficient means of support is present; and there is a competent ecclesiastical authority that approves and upholds the arrangement. Pertinent texts from the introductory articles of the faculties follow:

> The jurisdiction of the Military Vicar and his Chaplains.
>
> 1. This jurisdiction is *strictly personal* and may be exercised over their proper subjects any place on earth.
> 2. It extends to:
> a) All men of the armed forces belonging to the Army, Navy and Air Force who are in the active military service of the Federal Government or particular states;
> b) The wives, children, relatives and servants of the men of the armed forces who reside in the same house with them;
> c) All civilians staying within the limits of the military reservation;
> d) All religious—both men and sisters—also others, even lay persons, who are attached to military hospitals;
> e) All priests who are subjects of the Military Vicar, by reason of service with the armed forces.
> 3. It embraces parochial power in regard to their own proper subjects.[12]

As further strengthening the argument that the military chaplain of the United States may be looked upon as a personal pastor is the fact that he is charged with the *cura animarum* immediately upon his appointment.[13] Moreover, he possesses ordinary jurisdiction to hear confessions[14] and grants the matrimonial dispensations in accordance with the norms of canons 1043 and 1045, § 1, § 2.[15]

One cannot object that the American military chaplain must not be considered as a personal pastor for the reason that he is not

---

[12] *Letter to the Apostolic Delegate of the United States* (as translated by Bouscaren)—*Digest,* II, 587.

[13] *Military Faculties,* Part I, art. 1—Bouscaren, *Digest,* II, 589.

[14] *Military Faculties,* Part I, art. 13—Bouscaren, *Digest,* II, 595.

[15] *Military Faculties,* Part I, art. 19—Bouscaren, *Digest,* II, 601.

obliged to apply the *missa pro populo*. Inherently in his office he is obliged;[16] it is only through dispensation that he is freed from the obligation.[17]

6. The Code makes no specific provision regarding parishes which look to a diversity of rite as the determining factor for their membership. Since the Code is silent on that score, while it expressly mentions language, citizenship in a different country, family characteristics and personal qualities as bases for the constitution of separate parishes, authors generally agree that such parishes may be erected without an apostolic indult.[18]

It may here be pointed out, however, that in the Latin dioceses a diversity of rite rarely exists without an accompanying diversity of language or of citizenship. For that reason it could seem that, since an indult is required for the erection of national parishes, so too it is required for the erection of a parish of the Oriental rite. But since Orientals are not subject to the laws of the Code,[19] that restriction of their liberty cannot be placed upon them.[20]

An Oriental bishop, therefore, without consulting Rome can erect distinct parishes for his people, which parishes are based on a diversity of rite. Likewise a Latin bishop, if he has a sufficient number of Orientals subject to him, can on his own authority erect for them parishes which are distinct from the parishes of the Latin rite.[21]

A more valid reason, however, than the silence of Canon 216, § 4, seems to support this conclusion. The Church assigns a greater juridical importance to diversity of rite than to diversity of language, of citizenship, of family characteristics or of personal qualities. Diversity of rite, which entails a difference in the manner of administering the sacraments and of the exercise of public worship, cannot be as easily disregarded.[22] The law itself clearly shows

[16] Cappello, *Tractatus Canonico-Moralis de Sacramentis,* I, 560.

[17] *Regulae a Cappellanis Castrensibus Observandae,* n. 12—Bouscaren, *Digest,* II, 618.

[18] Maroto, *Institutiones Iuris Canonici,* II, 142; Claeys Bouuaert-Simenon, *Manuale Juris Canonici,* I, 218.

[19] Canon 1.

[20] Bernier, *De Patrimonio Paroeciali,* p. 38.

[21] Coronata, *Institutiones Iuris Canonici,* I, 367, footnote n. 4.

[22] Bernier, *op. cit., loc. cit.*

that it is the desire of the Church to preserve intact the Oriental rites.[23] The Roman Pontiffs have always shown a desire to protect the distinction in rites.[24] Since the need of an apostolic indult tends in practice to discourage the erection of Oriental parishes, no such requirement is laid down in the law.

7. In recent years the question of the essential nature of parishes for negroes has gained prominence. Racial diversity as a basis for the erection of a parish, as with diversity of rite, is not explicitly mentioned in canon 216, § 4. Perhaps the reason for the omission is the local nature of the negro problem. It is more or less confined to the United States.[25]

However, despite the omission of explicit reference to racial diversity, it can be established with certitude that the prescript of canon 216, § 4, does embrace parishes for colored people. Certainly such parishes cannot be territorial, for the nature of a territorial parish is such that it exists specifically as the *one* parish for the *general* population of a district, and as the one parish whose membership is assigned solely through domicile or quasi-domicile. If another parish is founded within the limits of a territorial parish, the second cannot also be primarily of a territorial nature. Diversity of language or of citizenship does not obtain in the case; the negro speaks the same language and has citizenship in the same country as the general population surrounding him. The factor for membership in the negro parish must therefore consist in the diversity between the white populace and the negroes as specifically distinguished personal groups. Parishes based on such a diversity are designated in canon 216, § 4, under the generic term "personal" parishes.[26]

Not always, however, are parishes for colored people personal

---

[23] Canons 98; 756; 1097, § 2.

[24] Vermeersch-Creusen, *Epitome Iuris Canonici,* I, 476.

[25] Connolly, *The Canonical Erection of Parishes,* p. 107.

[26] Bastnagel, "Is a Parish for Colored People a 'National' Parish?" *ER,* CVIII (1943), 385. Connolly (*The Canonical Erection of Parishes,* p. 108) states that they probably can be included under the wording *pro diversitate nationis.* He does not incline to the view that they can be termed personal parishes, inasmuch as they embrace a whole class of people, and the membership in them is too generic. The personal type of parish, he asserts, seems to embrace a more specific and individual membership.

parishes. At times, especially in the South, a territorially defined district may be solidly inhabited by a negro population. In that instance a parish which is designated for the use of all residing within the district must be considered simply as territorial. No apostolic indult would be necessary for the erection or for any change in the territorial boundaries of such a parish. If, however, the element of territory is only a secondary determining factor for membership, and racial characteristics serve as the primary factor, then the parish is a personal parish, and an apostolic indult must be sought for its erection and subsequent change.

Parishes erected for the Indians and Chinese would fall subject to the same general regulations. Such parishes, however, are more frequently territorial in nature than personal in character, for they are usually established in districts solely inhabited by these particular racial groups. Rarely are such parishes found in places besides Indian reservations and the "China Towns" of our larger cities.

ARTICLE 2. THE MINIMUM NUMBER OF THE FAITHFUL REQUIRED IN THE CONSTITUTION OF A PARISH

The question of the minimum number of people required in the constitution of a parish is left untouched by the Code. One must therefore be guided by the pre-Code doctrine and practice in this matter. The majority of the commentators held that at least ten Catholic families were required in the erection of a parish, but that a lesser number might suffice for the continued maintenance of parochial status. Some, however, inclined to the view the Protestant families could be included in the number. Others held that not ten families but ten persons sufficed. There were still others who simply insisted upon a mere plurality of families without indicating any definite number.[27]

How may one, then, arrive at an apodictic solution for the problem? Can it simply be stated that the majority opinion is to be followed—ten Catholic families are required for the erection of a parish, but a lesser number suffices for the maintenance of parochial status? Certainly that is a safe norm, but still it has not merited

[27] Cf. *supra*, Chapter III, Article 2, Section B.

any definitive canonical sanction. The few modern canonists who treat of the problem vary in their opinions, as did the pre-Code commentators.

Rossi simply states that ten families are required,[28] as does Bernier, who cites as his authority the ruling of canon, 6, 2°.[29] Connolly views the problem in the same light. While admitting that the German custom of including heretical as well as Catholic families in the number was doctrinally defensible, he rejects the practice on canonical grounds. In explanation he avers that heretics have obtained no exemption and are still subject to the pastor of their place of residence, but that canonically the ruling of c. 3, C. X, q. 3, seems to deal with actual rather than merely prospective families.[30] Cappello takes cognizance of the more common teaching of the ancient canonists, but simply states that in this day ten families are not required as a condition for valid erection of a parish. He states that in and of itself a lesser number could suffice.[31]

Recognizing that the weight of opinion among both the pre-Code and the post-Code authors requires a minimum of ten families for the erection of a parish, the present writer wholeheartedly concurs in their view. If an ordinary nevertheless erects a parish with a lesser number of families, his action must be looked upon as at most illicit, but not as invalid.

ARTICLE 3. THE MAXIMUM NUMBER OF THE FAITHFUL DESIRABLE IN A PARISH

As variant as are the opinions of the canonists in relation to the minimum number of people required in the constitution of a parish, they vary more widely in relation to the maximum desirable number of the faithful. Pope Pius VI (1775-1799) in a letter addressed to the bishops of France asserted that it was impossible for one pastor to adequately govern a flock of 6,000 souls. The brief entitled *Quod aliquantum* (March 10, 1791) was primarily directed against the civil authorities, who as a matter of practice

---

[28] *De Paroecia*, p. 21.

[29] *De Patrimonio Paroeciali*, p. 48.

[30] *The Canonical Erection of Parishes*, p. 60.

[31] *Summa Iuris Canonici*, I, 440.

were establishing parishes with memberships of no less than 6,000 souls.[32]

Leo XIII (1878-1903), in making a new division of the parishes in Rome, assigned no more than 3,000 parishioners to each.[33] And yet, when a pastor of the city of Ragusa, Italy, had recourse against the decree of his ordinary who had divided the Ragusa parish of 32,000 souls, the Sacred Congregation of the Council looked upon the case as not too unusual. The pastor maintained that with the help of his fifteen assistants he could give adequate spiritual care to all of his parishioners. The division decreed by the ordinary gave 13,485 souls to a new parish and 19,099 to the mother church. The Sacred Congregation upheld the decree of the ordinary, but neither counselled nor disapproved of further division.[34] In another case, presented on Jan. 21, 1905, the Sacred Congregation did not allow a division for the reason simply that the faithful numbered as many as 6,500 souls in a particular parish.[35]

Hence it can easily be seen that little is derivable from a consultation of the papal pronouncements and tribunal decisions, since they are so widely divergent and do not provide a definite norm. The bishop in erecting or dividing parishes is simply to be guided by his good judgment. Again, the spiritual welfare of souls is to be his prime consideration. Never should the number of parishioners be so large that their reasonable requests cannot be fulfilled by the clergy assigned to the church. Coronata looks upon 6,000 as a maximum number,[36] while De Meester seemed to favor 3,000;[37] but both are willing enough to admit that it is quite impossible to establish a norm that must be followed in every case.

---

[32] Claeys Bouuaert-Simenon, *Manuale Juris Canonici,* III, 161.

[33] De Meester, *Juris Canonici et Juris Canonico—civilis Compendium* (nova editio, 4 vols., Brugis, 1921-1928), III, 334, footnote n. 4 (hereafter cited *Compendium Juris Canonici*).

[34] S. C. C., *Syracusana,* 28 mart. 1903—*Fontes,* n. 4313.

[35] S. C. C., *Taurinen.—Fontes,* n. 4320.

[36] *Institutiones Iuris Canonici,* II, 379.

[37] *Op. cit.,* III, 334, footnote n. 4.

CHAPTER VI

The Office of Pastor

Article 1. Distinguishing Features of the Office

Throughout this study it has been stressed that it is the office of the pastor rather than the person of the pastor himself which must be considered among the inherent requisites in the constitution of a parish.[1] This view follows from the fact that a parish is a benefice. The argument stated in simple terms is this: An essential component part of a benefice is a sacred office, which in this case is that of the care of souls.[2] A benefice, moreover, is a moral person and therefore is of its nature perpetual.[3] For the reason that the parish is a benefice and of its nature perpetual, it does not cease to exist simply because the sacred office remains vacant. It is the pastoral office, therefore, rather than the person of the pastor which must be considered absolutely essential to the existence of a parish.

Yet the tenure of the office by an incumbent is a factor that cannot be completely divorced from the existence of the office. Certainly the office which entails the care of souls would be a useless thing unless in its normal state it were filled by a pastoral incumbent who exercises that care of souls. Canon 216, § 1, takes for granted the assignment to a parish of a particular rector, who is to fulfill that duty.

In the foregoing historical synopsis the distinguishing features of the office of pastor were discussed,[4] and they were pointed out as aids in determining the parochial status of a church. Little did the features vary with the advent of the Code in 1918. Chelodi[5] and

---

[1] Cf. *supra,* Chapter III, Article 2, Section C.

[2] Canon 1410.

[3] Canon 102, § 1.

[4] Cf. *supra,* Chapter III, Article 2, Section C.

[5] *Ius de Personis,* p. 350.

Cappello[6] simply listed the tokens of the parochial status of a church as they had been enumerated in pre-Code decrees: 1) the presence of a baptismal font in the church; 2) the power of the rector to assist at matrimony; 3) the obligation to apply the *Missa pro populo;* 4) the right of granting burial; 5) the right of distributing paschal Communion. They stressed, too, the already historically evident fact that if all these signs are present, then the church is most likely of a parochial character, but that if one or the other is lacking, the contrary cannot be affirmed immediately.

The present Code did not effect any modification of this list of features as related to the pastoral office, though it appears more firm than the pre-Code legislation in its insistence on a baptismal font for every parish church. Every parish church, so it decrees the while it revokes and reprobates all contrary statutes, privileges and customs, is to have a baptismal font. The legitimate cumulative rights as acquired in the past by some churches are however to stand.[7] (Previously the concession of cumulative baptismal rights to mother churches had been allowed.)

While according to the Code a pastor still retains his right to administer paschal Communion to his parishioners, the strict obligation to receive it from him is somewhat softened. In conformity with Pope Pius X's decree in 1912[8] the faithful are now merely urged to satisfy the precept of Easter Communion in their own parish churches. If they do satisfy it elsewhere, however, they are obliged to inform their proper pastor.[9]

Cavanaugh lists the obligation of the pastor to reserve the Blessed Sacrament as a further definitive indication of the parochial status of a church.[10] But inasmuch as the right to reserve the Blessed Sacrament is readily granted also to non-parochial churches,[11] and inasmuch as there cannot be any binding obliga-

---

[6] *Summa Iuris Canonici,* I, 442.

[7] Canon 774, § 1.

[8] S. C. C., *Decretum,* 28 nov.—*AAS,* IV (1912), 726.

[9] Canon 859, § 3.

[10] *The Reservation of the Blessed Sacrament,* The Catholic University of America Canon Law Studies, n. 40 (Washington, D. C.: The Catholic University of America, 1927), p. 23.

[11] Pont. Comm. ad Int. C. I. C., 20 maii 1923—*AAS,* XVI (1923), 115.

tion when a parish is erected without a church, the reservation of the Blessed Sacrament can hardly be regarded as betokening the parochial character of the church in question.

ARTICLE 2. THE PASTOR

Although, as has been stated, a parish can exist without a pastor, in its normal state it is to be taken for granted that an incumbent will fill the pastoral office. Canon 451, § 1, defines the pastor as an individual priest or a moral person to whom a parish has been given *in titulum* with the care of souls to be exercised under the authority of the local ordinary. Some elements of this definition call for explanation. A clear understanding of the definition does much to clarify the distinctions existing between pastors and parochial vicars, priests in charge of mission churches, etc.

1. Of vital importance in considering the implications of the definition is insistence upon the words *in titulum*. An exact rendition of the words in English is difficult. Woywod (1880-1941) simply stated "The phrase *'in titulum'* may be translated 'with rightful possession,' designating the office, rights and duties of the legal holder of the parish."[12] Augustine (1872-1943) was more explicit and detailed, although he presented his explanation of the phrase in somewhat involved language:

> A title may be defined as 'the legitimate cause of possessing what otherwise does not belong to one.' . . . To hold a parish in title, or the title to a parish, therefore, means to be the owner or possessor thereof. However no *parochus* can be styled the owner or proprietor of a parish. We might say that the bishop is the proprietor of all the parishes in his diocese, especially if he holds them in fee simple. But here 'title' must be restricted to possession by a legitimate cause. By holding a parish, then, 'animi et corporis detentione et iuris adminiculo,' a priest comes into possession of a parish; and this suffices to say that the parish was given him 'in title.'[13]

---

[12] *A Practical Commentary on the Code of Canon Law* (5. ed., 2 vols., New York: Joseph F. Wagner, 1939), I, 160.

[13] *A Commentary on the New Code of Canon Law* (8 vols., Vol. II, 3. ed., St. Louis: Herder and Co., 1919), II, 510.

Bouscaren simply translates the phrase "in his own right" and offers little further in explanation.[14] A true pastor, therefore, is one who, besides having the administration of a church, possesses a strict legal and vested right to the office of pastor. He exercises the care of souls in his own right, and functions not as a mere delegate of the bishop or of any other person.

In determining the parochial status of a church, it is extremely important for one to take into consideration these attributes of the pastoral office. For it is often only the fact that a parish is conferred upon a pastor *in titulum* which distinguishes him from other priests assigned to the care of churches. For example, the distinction between him and the persons mentioned in canon 451, § 2, 2°, namely, the parochial vicars, results only from that fact. The parochial vicars have full parochial powers and can be compared to the pastor in every other way; but they have been granted their churches *in administrationem* only, and not *in titulum*.[15]

Likewise the distinction between pastors and assistant pastors in charge of mission churches in our country rests upon the same fact. In sparsely settled dioceses, it has often been found necessary to erect at some distance from the principal church stations for the proper care of the pastoral needs of souls. At times as many as two or three subsidiary churches are demanded in view of the existing circumstances. Inasmuch as the pastor is kept occupied with affairs at the principal church, the stations are oftentimes assigned to a curate, who there by decree of the ordinary exercises the care of souls.

The stations have a determinate district, a distinct group of people and a particular church. Thus they seemingly possess all the necessary qualifications for a true parochial status; but since the assistants are assigned to these churches *in administrationem* only, the mission stations are nothing more than outposts of the parish church,[16] and their rectors are merely *vicarii cooperatores*.[17]

---

[14] *Canon Law, A Text and Commentary,* p. 189.

[15] S. C. C., *Blesensis,* 12 nov. 1927—*AAS,* XX (1928), 84.

[16] Cavanaugh, *The Reservation of the Blessed Sacrament,* p. 24.

[17] S. C. C., *Wratislavien.,* 13 iul. 1918—*AAS,* XI (1919), pp. 46-51. In this case presented to the Sacred Congregation of the Council there are described three types of so-called mission churches. Unless one give careful attention

2. Important, too, in considering the Code's definition of a pastor is the distinction drawn between the "physical" and the "moral" person to whom a parish may be conferred. If the pastor is a physical person, he must be a priest, and he must, as authors put it, *ex iure et facto* exercise the care of souls.[18] In that instance he is known as an actual pastor.

But the title of pastor can also be vested in moral persons, such as ecclesiastical corporations, chapters, or religious orders. As moral or juridical personalities these cannot actually exercise the care of souls, and in consequence the law decrees that they must provide a vicar who will perform that duty.[19]

In the pre-Code law there was some question whether the term "pastor" was really applicable to such corporate institutes. Wernz (1842-1914) held this designation as not applicable to them, though he acknowledged their holding of the parish in title.[20] Bouix (1808-1870) had held the same opinion.[21]

In the present law there can be no doubt that any moral person or corporate institute which holds a parish in title is also to be regarded as the pastor of that parish. In this country, however, the uniting of a parish with such a juridic entity is not a matter of common occurrence. It is effected only when by indult the Holy See has approved the union of a parish with some collegiate

---

in studying the distinctions between the three, confusion is inevitable. The first type described (in which the rector was pronounced a true pastor and his church a true parish) is not a description of mission churches as they exist in our country. Kaiser, in an article entitled "Ecclesiastical Legislation on the *Missa pro Populo*" (*ER,* LXI (1919), 369-371), wrongly asserted that the two are identical. He evidently neglected to consider that these churches were described as existing in areas where there were no parish churches upon which they could possibly be dependent. The so-called "curates" in charge of these stations had no connection with a principal church whatsoever. Since the "curates" could not possibly be described as *vicarii cooperatores,* and since it was not possible to argue that the so-called mission stations pertained to some other parish, or that they had another pastor besides the rector of the mission, it was decided that they merely had the name of "mission stations," but in actuality were true parishes.

[18] Rossi, *De Paroecia,* p. 65.

[19] Canon 471, § 1.

[20] *Ius Decretalium,* II, n. 821.

[21] *Tractatus de Parocho,* p. 179.

moral person. Through such a full union the moral person becomes vested with the title of pastor, and then must exercise the care of souls in the parish by means of a vicar.

There is also possible the effecting of a less complete union, in consequence of which a priest of the diocese is appointed for the care of souls in the parish and receives compensation for his services, but the revenues of the parish yield in whole or in part to the moral person. Although this arrangement, for which there likewise is needed an indult of the Holy See, resembles that of the full union in some respects, the moral person is not constituted as the pastor in title, and hence the one who is appointed for the care of souls truly holds such a parish in title as its pastor.

3. The care of souls connected with the office of pastor received some consideration in the introductory article of this chapter. But for the purpose of emphasizing certain points a further discussion seems in place here. In differentiating the status of a pastor from that of other priests who in a dependent capacity exercise the care of souls one must first of all note that his power is an ordinary power in that it is inherently attached to the office itself. When a priest is granted the title of pastor, he obtains all requisite pastoral jurisdiction in his own name, and not simply as a deputy who functions in the name of the bishop.[22] His power is such that the bishop cannot detach it from the conferred pastoral office or limit it in such a fashion that it becomes but a semblance of the power that is vested in the pastoral office.[23]

Thus the difference between a pastor and other priests who in a dependent capacity exercise the care of souls is easily discernible. The pastor exercises his power in his own name and in virtue of his appointment to the office; the others exercise their power in the name of another and by way of committed delegation. Accordingly the pastor can hear confessions and preach without the need of any specific act of approbation when he exercises these acts within the sphere of his pastoral office; the others cannot exercise these acts unless they have received a specific approbation for the performance of them.

---

[22] Rossi, *De Paroecia*, p. 71.

[23] Sipos, *Enchiridion Iuris Canonici* (Pecs, 1926), p. 294.

4. While it is essential to the pastorate that its incumbent minister to his flock in his own name, it must nevertheless be stressed that he is subject to the ordinary of the place and fulfills his duties under the authority of the bishop. The pastor's power does not reflect the possession of a jurisdiction that extends to the external as well as the internal forum. It extends primarily and normally to the internal forum. It is only by a special provision of the law that pastors have a very limited jurisdiction in the external forum. They may under urgent conditions dispense from certain matrimonial impediments,[24] and they may also in particular instances dispense individual persons or families in their parish from the law regarding the observance of feast days, or of fast or abstinence, or of all of these in the presence of just cause.[25] Moreover, pastors have in the external forum what is often referred to as "domestic power." They may give precepts, warn, correct, use moderate coercion, and in general watch over their subjects both spiritually and temporally.[26] Always, however, this power is to be used within circumscribed limits and in due subordinate relation to the authority of the local ordinary, whose possession of this power is of a full and primary character.

A. *Unicity in the Office of Pastor*

The question regarding the character of unicity in the pastoral office as essential to the parochial status of a church was at one time the subject of lengthy canonical discussion. The question, "What is required that a church be designated as parochial?" consistently evoked from the classicists the answer, "It is required that the church have a rector who serves in that capacity to the exclusion of others, one and all."[27] Schmalzgrueber (1663-1735) was particularly emphatic. To stress the point, he delved into historical arguments. He cited the epistles of St. Jerome and had recourse to the *Decree of Gratian*. He furthermore quoted a mem-

[24] Canons 1044, 1045.

[25] Canon 1245, § 1.

[26] Bouscaren-Ellis, *Canon Law, A Text and Commentary*, p. 189; Sipos, *Enchiridion Iuris Canonici*, p. 294.

[27] Cf. *supra*, Chapter III, footnote n. 73.

orable canon attributed to a Council of Reims (630): "Just as a woman cannot have two husbands or one body two heads, so a church cannot have two presbyters."[28]

Later canonists treated the matter in a lighter vein, and though most of them admitted that it was contrary to the mind of the church that two pastors should rule over the same parochial church, yet they asserted that the presence of two pastors at one parochial church did not substantially affect its parochial status.[29] Bouix went so far as to state that such an arrangement was not contrary to the canons.[30]

Regardless of what the law may have called for in pre-Code times, there did exist some parishes in which two or more pastors exercised the care of souls. Rossi reported a case in which a parish in Paris was under the spiritual care of three pastors and later under two.[31]

An arrangement whereby a parish is held in title by the canonical pastor but is actually administered by a parochial vicar, is not of course forbidden by the present law. Nor is it absolutely forbidden, when necessity urges, that one parish church constitute the parochial seat for two distinct parishes and two pastors.[32] But most certainly it is not possible in present times that two pastors could legitimately rule over one and the same parish with mutually equal authority. Canon 460, § 2, specifically states that for each parish there can be but one pastor who is held responsible there for the care of souls. The law applies with equal force to parishes that were erected prior to the Code,[33] and its reprobation of all customs to the contrary precludes also the formation of contrary customs in the future.[34]

---

[28] *Ius Ecclesiasticum Universum,* Lib. III, tit. 29, n. 4. Cf. can. 9 of the Council of Reims—Mansi, X, 603.

[29] Wernz, *Ius Decretalium,* II, n. 821, p. 1030, footnote n. 15.

[30] *Tractatus de Parocho,* p. 187.

[31] *De Paroecia,* p. 80. Cf. S. C. C., *Mandelen.,* 17 mart. 1917—*AAS,* IX (1917), 343-350.

[32] Coronata, *Institutiones Iuris Canonici,* I, 578.

[33] Pontificia Commissio Interpretationis (P.C.I.), 14 iul. 1922—*AAS,* XIV (1922), 526.

[34] The prescript applies, so Vermeersch contended, merely to those parishes in which the actual care of souls is exercised cumulatively by more than one

B. *Perpetuity in the Office of Pastor*

Perpetuity with reference to the pastoral office can be understood in two distinct ways. Objective perpetuity has reference to the pastoral office itself. If the parish is such that it will not of itself cease to exist, but will lapse from existence solely in consequence of a decree of the competent ecclesiastical authority or through some other positive provisions of the law, then the pastoral office in relation to that parish is said to possess objective perpetuity. Subjective perpetuity relates to the continued and abiding incumbency in the pastoral office. If the parish has been conferred upon a pastor for his lifetime, so that he cannot be removed except with the use of the legal formalities enacted in canons 2147-2156, then the pastoral office is said to possess subjective perpetuity. The question now arises: Must both of these forms of perpetuity attach to the pastoral office before it can serve as the constitutive element of a parish?

The Council of Trent had pointed to perpetuity in the pastor's incumbency as a characteristic that was desired for the pastoral office.[35] Moreover, since the post-Tridentine canonists recognized a parish as a benefice, they insisted on both objective and subjective perpetuity as an essential requirement in the pastoral office.[36]

Nevertheless, there continued to exist many parishes whose pastors were not permanent incumbents in the pastoral office they held. After the French Revolution, in France and the adjoining regions, parishes whose pastoral incumbents were removable at the will of the bishop became the rule rather than the exception. A short time later this departure from ecclesiastical discipline received acknowledgment and approval from the Holy See.[37] It is

---

pastor. Although an arrangement by which a number of pastors rule a parish by turns, e.g., one after the other in alternating weeks, seems also to be excluded, he stated that this prohibition cannot be proved conclusively from the text of canon 460. Nevertheless the Sacred Congregation of the Council frowns upon such a practice.—*Epitome Iuris Canonici,* I, 390.

[35] Sess. XXIV, *de ref.,* c. 13.

[36] Schmalzgrueber, Lib. III, tit. 29, pars II, n. 8; Reiffenstuel, Lib. III, tit. 5, n. 8. Cf. Smith, *Elements of Ecclesiastical Law* (3 vols., Vol. I, 9. ed., New York, 1893), I, 114.

[37] Wernz, *Ius Decretalium,* II, n. 821.

not surprising that the later pre-Code authors, while insisting on objective perpetuity, simply stated that subjective perpetuity in the pastoral office, even though desirable, was not essentially required in the constitution of a parish.[38]

The present law leaves no question in the matter. Since every parish is a moral person, which of its nature is of a permanent character,[39] the office which serves its needs must likewise have permanence, that is, it must possess objective perpetuity. The concomitant element of subjective perpetuity in the tenure of that office, though it may of course be present, is nevertheless not required. This was stated explicitly in a decree of the Sacred Congregation of the Consistory,[40] and the law itself provides for the removability of pastors. Canon 454, which deals with the varying degrees of stability, distinguishes pastors who are irremovable, simply removable, or, if they are members of a religious community, removable at the discretion of the ordinary. The Code manifestly favors the higher degree of stability, since it declares that without an apostolic indult a pastoral office whose incumbent is irremovable may not be declared to be an office whose incumbent is made removable; moreover, that a bishop may convert a pastoral office whose incumbent is removable into a pastoral office whose incumbent becomes irremovable; and further that the incumbents in the pastoral offices of new parishes are to be considered irremovable unless the bishop expressly decrees that they are appointed as removable incumbents.[41]

---

[38] De Angelis, *Praelectiones Iuris Canonici* (2. ed., 5 vols., Romae, 1908), I, 54; Bouix, *Tractatus de Parocho*, p. 168.

[39] Cf. Mundy, *The Union of Parishes*, pp. 32-33.

[40] *Decretum*, 1 aug. 1919—*AAS*, XI (1919), 346.

[41] Canon 454, § 3.

CHAPTER VII

The Parish Church and an Adequate Endowment

Inasmuch as the question regarding the necessity of a parochial church for the constitution of a parish cannot easily be separated from a discussion of the sufficient endowment required for a parish, it seems preferable to treat these related topics in one and the same chapter.

ARTICLE 1. THE PARISH CHURCH

In its normal state every parish should have a parish church. The present Code leaves no doubt about the matter. Canon 216, § 1, plainly states that to each territorial division of a diocese a special (*peculiaris*) church is to be assigned; and parochial legislation throughout the Code seems to take for granted the existence of a church proper to each parish. A baptismal font is required for every parochial church;[1] the faithful are urged to satisfy the precept of paschal Communion in their own parishes;[2] the Blessed Sacrament must be reserved in all parochial or quasi-parochial churches;[3] pastors are given faculties to bless the sacred furnishings of their own churches.[4]

Nowhere in the Code is there any distinct legislation with reference to parishes which are minus a proper parochial church. Yet the authors are in unanimous agreement that the church itself must not be looked upon as absolutely essential. A parish, they simply state, can exist without a church of its own.[5] By what au-

[1] Canon 774, § 1.

[2] Canon 859, § 3.

[3] Canon 1265, § 2.

[4] Canon 1304.

[5] Connolly, *The Canonical Erection of Parishes*, p. 5; Ciesluk, *National Parishes*, p. 5; Coronata, *Institutiones Iuris Canonici*, I, 367. Claeys Bouuaert-Simenon (*Manuale Juris Canonici*, I, 217) state that the exceptional arrangement whereby one church serves two parishes can be applied only to mission territories.

thority is this common opinion ventured? The authors cite no canons of the Code on the matter, but rely (and with justification) on various pre-Code decisions issued by the Sacred Congregations.

The Council of Trent enacted legislation that pointed to the necessity of a parochial church. Canon 216, § 1, in its content is similar to that legislation.[6] The Sacred Congregation of the Council, however, declared that the Tridentine legislation was not to be interpreted with a rigid and unbending literalness, so that if necessity pleaded for the contrary, then one church could serve several pastors in ruling distinct groups of the faithful.[7] The ruling of this decree was restated in a number of like decrees, the latest of which specifically declared that a parish could be constituted with full parochial rights and obligations even though it did not have a church of its own.[8] Since canons which restate the earlier law are to be interpreted according to the authority of that law,[9] the interpretation of the Sacred Congregation of the Council maintains its force and application also for the present.

Further justification for the opinion is hardly required, but certainly an argument may be derived from canon 1415, § 3, which states that it is not forbidden to erect a parish or a quasi-parish when a sufficient endowment cannot be established. The very definition of a sufficient endowment is that which is adequate of itself for the sustentation of the clergy, the maintenance of the church in which the benefice is erected, and for other current expenses.[10] Certainly, if the faithful are financially unable to provide for the upkeep of a pastor and a church, no prudent person would allow them the construction of a church to be made subject to an unpayable debt. And yet, if necessity demands it, the erection of a parish or a quasi-parish for these people is not thereby forbidden.

The bishop, after determining that the necessary minimum support (not necessarily a sufficient endowment) will be had from at least some other source,[11] simply defines territorial limits for a

[6] Sess. XXIV, *de ref.*, c. 13.

[7] *Hispalen.*, 25 ian. 1895—*ASS*, XXVII (1895), 10.

[8] Cf. *supra*, Chapter III, footnote n. 57.

[9] Canon 6, 2°.

[10] Coronata, *Institutiones Iuris Canonici*, II, 367.

[11] Cf. *infra*, Article 2.

section of his diocese,[12] appoints a pastor to govern the faithful residing within that territory, and from that moment a new parish comes into existence. The spiritual care of the faithful may be arranged in one of three ways: 1) The newly-created pastor may seek a temporary building in which to perform with the proper permission the liturgical functions and to administer the sacraments to his flock; 2) the care of souls may be entrusted to a neighboring pastor, while the proper pastor arranges for a temporary structure or collects funds for the construction of a new church;[13] 3) the newly-created pastor, by arrangement of the ordinary with the neighboring pastor, fulfills his pastoral duties through the facilities offered by a neighboring church, while plans for the construction of his own church are in the making.

Thus it is that the church building itself may not be listed among the absolutely essential elements of a parish. Must there, however, always be present the intention to erect a church? It can be stated apodictically that there must.[14] The law, as has been pointed out, does not conceive of a parish without a church of its own apart from an exceptional provision in unusual circumstances. Parochial legislation is such that it cannot be completely observed without the existence of a church building. It is not possible, therefore, that an ordinary allow the erection of a parish when he knows that a church will never be constructed. Even though the future date be undetermined, the intention to erect a church must be present.

ARTICLE 2. THE SUFFICIENT ENDOWMENT

A. *A Discussion of Canon 1415, § 3*

Canon 1409. Beneficium ecclesiasticum est ens iuridicum a competente ecclesiastica auctoritate in perpetuum constitutum seu erectum, constans officio

[12] If division or dismemberment of a parish is entailed in his act, the ordinary must abide by the prescriptions of canon 1427.

[13] In such circumstances the office of the pastor exists *in habitu* as distinguished from an office which exists *in exercitio*. The pastor retains the right to administer to his parishioners, but the exercise of that right is temporarily suspended. Cf. Ciesluk, *National Parishes*, p. 5.

[14] Mundy, *The Union of Parishes*, p. 10.

sacro et iure percipiendi reditus ex dote officio adnexos.

Canon 1410. Dotem beneficii constituunt sive bona quorum proprietas est penes ipsum ens iuridicum, sive certae et debitae praestationes alicuius familiae vel personae moralis, sive certae et voluntariae fidelium oblationes, quae ad beneficii rectorem spectent, sive iura, ut dicitur, stolae intra fines taxationis dioecesanae vel legitimae consuetudinis, sive chorales distributiones, exclusa tertia earundem parte, si omnes reditus beneficii choralibus distributionibus constent.

Canon 1415, § 1. Beneficia ne erigantur, nisi constet ea stabilem et congruam dotem habere, ex qua reditus perpetuo percipiantur ad normam can. 1410.

§ 3. Non prohibetur tamen (Ordinarius), ubi congrua dos constituti nequeat, paroecias aut quasiparoecias erigere, si prudenter praevideat ea quae necessaria sunt aliunde non defutura.

Paragraph three of canon 1415 states that an ordinary is not forbidden to erect parishes or quasi-parishes, even though an adequate endowment cannot be established, provided that he foresees that the necessaries for support will be forthcoming from some other source. At first glance the wording of the canon seems to be evident, and yet it has given rise to many practical difficulties. If a parish is established without an adequate endowment, does this mean that it cannot be considered a benefice? Or, rather, does the canon establish an exception to the general law, i.e. that a parish even without a sufficient endowment retains its beneficial nature? Must emphasis be placed upon the word *congrua,* so that an endowment at least in the minutest quantity is still required by the law? Finally, must the words *congrua dos* be limited in their interpretation to an adequate endowment in the strict sense of the term (property or invested capital), so that a sufficient endowment in the form of voluntary offerings of the faithful, stole fees, etc., is still required by the final clause of the canon?

A solution of these problems is most urgent. The opinions of the authors are as widely divergent as the possibilities in the interpretation of the canon. Bernier takes the view that a parish may be established without a sufficient endowment, but in that contingency it must not be looked upon as a benefice. He is aware, he states, of the private response of Cardinal Gasparri (president of the Pontifical Commission for the Authentic Interpretation of the Code) to the Apostolic Delegate of the United States, in which it is stated: "A parish is always an ecclesiastical benefice according to c. 1411, 5°, whether it has the proper endowment (resources or revenue) as described and defined in c. 1410, or even if lacking such endowment (resources or revenue) it be erected according to the provisions of c. 1415, § 3."[15] Bernier, however, denies that the Cardinal was acting in his official capacity as president of the Pontifical Commission, or that he intended to give an authentic interpretation of canon 1415, § 3.

Supporting his argument, he provides a quotation from a decision of the Sacred Congregation of the Council,[16] in which the parochial status of so called "mission stations" was declared: *"Neque obiici potest quod huiusmodi stationes in beneficium erectae non sint . . . etenim id quoque non obstaret, quominus paroeciae essent dicendae ad tramitem can. 1415, § 3."*[17]

Golden in his study argues that the parishes erected under the provisions of canon 1415, § 3, must be considered benefices despite the fact that they have no endowment. He states:

> The only reason for thinking that the parishes of canon 1415 are not benefices is that they have not the required endowment, but even that is not conclusive, as the very mention of them under the subject of benefices may be sufficient to conclude that they are benefices by exception to the general rule. When canon 1412 speaks of certain institutions and offices which have a certain similarity to benefices, without being true benefices, it does not mention this species of parish, and this may be used as an additional argument in favor of their status as benefices.[18]

---

[15] *Letter of the Apostolic Delegate, United States,* 10 Nov., 1922—Bouscaren, *Digest,* I, 150.

[16] *Wratislavien,* 13 iul. 1918—*AAS,* XI (1919), 50.

[17] Bernier, *De Patrimonio Paroeciali,* pp. 55-56.

[18] *Parochial Benefices,* p. 20.

Vermeersch[19] and Claeys Bouuaert-Simenon[20] seem to be of the same opinion as Golden.

The majority of the authors, however, are reluctant to agree with this viewpoint. The existence of a benefice without an endowment, they state, seems to be repugnant to the very nature of a benefice.[21] Nevertheless, the same authors are unwilling to declare that parishes which according to canon 1415, § 3, have been erected apart from a sufficient endowment are not benefices, and so through devious means attempt to explain the apparent contradiction.

De Meester,[22] Woywod[23] and Ayrinhac[24] interpret the expression *"congrua dos,"* which occurs in canon 1415, § 3, as referring to an endowment in the strict sense of the term—property or invested capital, the revenues from which accrue to the beneficiary. The *"necessaria aliunde non defutura"* of the final clause is interpreted as referring to revenues which will come from an endowment in the form of voluntary offerings of the faithful, stole fees, etc. Hence they seemingly infer that canon 1415, § 3, contains no actual dispensation from the necessity of having an adequate endowment in the erection of a parish, but simply a dispensation from the normal requirement that an adequate endowment in the form of property or in the form of invested capital be had. Cappello apparently concurs with this opinion when he declares that "the erection of a parish or of a quasi-parish, though a sufficient endowment is lacking, is not prohibited if it is prudently foreseen that those things which are necessary will not be lacking from some other source, v.g., from stole fees or the offerings of the faithful." He states that in this case the endowment exists in prospect rather than in actual fact *"in spe non autem actu,"* and that a guaranteed future existence of the endowment suffices.[25]

Coronata, in the opinion of this writer, offers the best solution

---

[19] *Epitome Iuris Canonici,* II, 526.

[20] *Manuale Juris Canonici,* III, 136.

[21] Coronata, *Institutiones Iuris Canonici,* II, 366.

[22] *Compendium Juris Canonici,* III, 326.

[23] *A Practical Commentary on the Code of Canon Law,* II, 138.

[24] *Administrative Legislation,* p. 317.

[25] *Summa Iuris Canonici,* II, 514.

for the problem. He observes that the Code in canon 1415, § 3, does not completely dispense from an endowment, but only from an *adequate* endowment. If an endowment in even the minutest quantity is lacking, then it is forbidden to erect a parish or a quasi-parish. In favor of his argument he cites a decree of the Sacred Congregation of the Consistory;[26] "If . . . the absolute want of an endowment makes it inadvisable to erect certain churches into parishes, let these churches be considered as subsidiary churches or chaplaincies within the boundaries of an existing parish upon which they shall remain dependent, until they can become parishes themselves."[27] Coronata's opinion seems to be the only one that duly reconciles the seeming contradictions between canons 1409, 1410, 1415, § 1, and 1415, § 3, the various decrees emanating from the Sacred Congregations, and the private response of Cardinal Gasparri to the Apostolic Delegate of the United States.

The denial by Bernier of the fact that parishes erected in accordance with canon 1415, § 3, are benefices directly contradicts Cardinal Gasparri's reply to the Apostolic Delegate. Bernier's statement that the Cardinal was not acting in his official capacity as the President of the Pontifical Commission for the Authentic Interpretation of the Code is a gratuitous one. The response, it is to be remembered, came as the result of a query addressed not to the person of the Cardinal but to the Pontifical Commission.[28]

Golden, in proclaiming that the parishes of canon 1415 are benefices even though they have no endowment whatsoever, not only contradicts canon 1409 but also the very nature and the whole history of the benefice.[29]

The view propounded by De Meester, Cappello, Woywod and Ayrinhac seems to be contradictory to canon 1410. This canon draws no distinction between an endowment in the strict sense and an endowment in the wide sense. It simply declares that the endowment of a benefice consists either of the goods owned by the

---

[26] *Declaratio,* 1 aug. 1919—*AAS,* XI (1919), 346.

[27] *Institutiones Iuris Canonici,* II, 366.

[28] "Under date of 20 March, 1921, I [the Apostolic Delegate] submitted to the said Commission the following question. . . ."—*Letter of the Apostolic Delegate, U. S.,* 10 Nov. 1922—Bouscaren, *Digest,* I, 150.

[29] Cf. Mundy, *The Union of Parishes,* pp. 20-21.

benefice itself as a juridical entity, or of certain and definite obligatory payments of some family or moral person, or of definite voluntary offerings of the faithful, or of stole fees, or of choral distributions. Thus the income accruing from any of these sources is placed in the same category. Hence, under the present law, the distinction drawn by the authors between a strict endowment and an endowment in the wide sense of the term is not warranted by canon 1410. There seems to be no authority for stating that the expression *"congrua dos,"* as occurring in the earlier part of canon 1415, § 3, refers to property or invested capital, whereas the phrase *"necessaria aliunde non defutura"* in the latter part of canon 1415, § 3, has reference to income accruing from stole fees, donations and voluntary offerings of the faithful.[30]

There seems to be only a few worthy objections to the viewpoint of Coronata. Bernier's quotation from a decree of the Sacred Congregation of the Council deserves primary mention: "Nor can it be objected that these stations may not have been erected into benefices . . . for notwithstanding that, they might be called parishes according to the concept of canon 1415, 3." This seems to imply a denial of the fact that the parishes which have been erected in accordance with canon 1415, § 3, are benefices, and yet one cannot arrive at that conclusion decisively, for the full quotation from the Sacred Congregation reads: "Nor can it be objected that these stations may not have been erected into benefices *or that they may not have the required endowment,* concerning which nothing was stated in the documents of the case; for notwithstanding that, they might be called parishes, etc. . . ."[31] Did the Congregation while defending the parochial status of the "mission stations" primarily seek to answer the objection to the possible lack of an adequate endowment? It seems to this writer that it did. If it had denied that parishes erected in accordance with canon 1415, § 3, are benefices, as Bernier holds, then Cardinal Gasparri's later response

[30] Cf. Pistocchi (*De Re Beneficiali* [Taurini, 1928], p. 52), who states: "Antequam dos constituatur, stante necessitate, Ordinarius paroecias vel quasi-paroecias potest erigere, dummodo tamen constet, si nequit congrua dos constituti, quae tamen sunt necessaria aliunde (*non ex dote*) non defutura."—Italics inserted.

[31] *Wratislavien.*, 13 iul. 1918—*AAS*, XI (1919), 50. Italics inserted.

to the Apostolic Delegate of the United States would have implied a contradiction of the earlier declaration of the Sacred Congregation, which is surely not readily to be assumed.

A second objection arises from a consideration of those parishes which will depend upon the voluntary offerings of the faithful as an endowment. At the time of the erection of such parishes there is ordinarily no actual endowment on hand. How can this be reconciled with Coronata's opinion that a minimum endowment is still required under the prescript of canon 1415, § 3? The explanation does not seem particularly difficult. It is true that in such cases the endowment in the form of voluntary offerings is ordinarily not in the hands of those about to erect the parish. The free-will offerings have not as yet been presented, yet there is present more than a mere hope of receiving them. Certitude is had that at the first request they will be presented. It cannot be said that such offerings have no existence whatsoever. They exist in the hands of the faithful and, given the occasion, the faithful make them a part of the beneficial endowment of the parish.

Hence this writer avers that, while a parish or a quasi-parish may be erected without a sufficient endowment, an endowment in at least some minute quantity is required. If even that is lacking, if no offerings or stole fees whatsoever may be expected from the faithful, then the erection of a parish or a quasi-parish is prohibited.

When a parish or a quasi-parish is erected with some minute, though not sufficient, endowment, the deficiency becomes suppliable through a missionary fund[32] or through temporary relief provided by a private individual. Another alternative is the uniting of a non-parochial benefice, in which the care of souls is not involved, with the newly-erected parish, as could be done if an immense Mass foundation had been constituted as a benefice. A further possible solution could derive from the spontaneously given consent of the incumbent to live on his own patrimony.

Thus it is that an endowment must be considered essential in the erection of a parish. But could a once created parochial benefice lose its endowment completely (e.g. through the withdrawal of

[32] The aid offered in the United States by the Catholic Church Extension Society, which builds churches and grants subsidies to pastors, serves as a good example.

support by the civil government) and still maintain its status as a benefice? It becomes immediately evident that it can. A benefice is a moral person.[33] A moral person is by its very nature perpetual; it becomes extinct only through suppression by legitimate authority, or if it has ceased to manifest any active existence over a period of one hundred years.[34] Since neither of these conditions obtain in the case, it must be affirmed that a parochial benefice, even though it loses its endowment, nevertheless maintains its status as a benefice and continues in existence as such.[35]

Therefore, while an endowment must be listed among the essential elements for the erection of a parish or a quasi-parish, it cannot be considered anything more than an accessory element which serves for the continued maintenance of the parish or the quasi-parish.

B. *The Various Means of Support*

Parishes erected under the provision of canon 1415, § 3, will of course be the exception rather than the rule. Normally an adequate endowment in one form or another is to be expected. An adequate endowment is a canonical expression which is subject to various interpretations. It has been understood as designating the lowest sum proper for the yearly income of a cleric assigned to a benefice,[36] but the better opinion is that a suitable endowment is one which, besides furnishing a proper income for the beneficiary, will suffice for the erection and maintenance of the permanent parochial fixtures, such as the church, the parochial residence, and the school, and will also provide a sufficient income for the proper conduct of sacred worship.[37]

It has, of course, been impossible to fix a determinate sum in the Church's universal law. The amount of income necessary for a parish will vary from place to place. Therefore the determination of what constitutes an adequate endowment must be left to

[33] Canon 99.

[34] Canon 102, § 1.

[35] Cappello, *Summa Iuris Canonici,* II, 514.

[36] Golden, *Parochial Benefices,* p. 18.

[37] Coronata, *Institutiones Iuris Canonici,* II, 367; Connolly, *The Canonical Erection of Parishes,* p. 76.

the judgment of the bishop.[38] Whatever amount is decided as necessary, it must be certain and perpetual, and not subject to any danger of loss, for the endowment is established for the maintenance of a juridical institute, which in law is acknowledged as having permanency of existence.[39]

The sources of endowment for a parish are enumerated in canons 1410 and 1427, § 3. The first mentioned in canon 1410 and the first in the historical order is the property and the goods which by ownership belong to the benefice as a juridical entity. This is the oldest and the classic definition of an endowment. As early as the fifth century the bishop had begun to grant the use of real estate offerings as one means of support for individual priests who had charge of particular churches. By the sixth century these concessions had become the universal practice. Finally, besides the administration the very dominion of the property was transferred to each church, so that the incumbent of the parochial benefice depended solely on the revenues accruing from this source.[40] With the passage of time even movable goods, such as bonds or invested capital, came to be classified as an endowment strictly so called.[41]

Since this method of support establishes financial stability and leaves little uncertainty concerning the future security of a parish, the Church favors the establishment of such endowments.[42] Many disagreeable features of church support, as they exist especially in the United States, could then be dispensed with. Pew rent, door collections and assessments would become entirely unnecessary.

Certain and obligatory payments made by families or moral per-

---

[38] *Conc. Trident.*, sess. XXI, *de ref.*, c. 4. Cf. Canon 1415, § 1, in which a demand is made for a suitable endowment, but with no specification of a determinate sum.

[39] S. C. C., *Quebecen.*, 14 iul. 1917—*AAS*, X (1918), 196; S. C. C., *Squillacen.*, 14 dec. 1895—*Analecta Ecclesiastica*, III (1895), 487. Cf. Canon 1415, § 1.

[40] Mundy, *The Union of Parishes*, p. 21.

[41] Ayrinhac, *Administrative Legislation*, p. 317; Pistocchi, *De Re Beneficiali*, p. 17.

[42] Although modern methods of diocesan administration call for certain restrictions to be placed on the rights of those who endow churches (patrons), the Church is still very liberal in its concessions to them. Cf. cans. 1417, § 1; 1450; 1455.

sons constitute a second means of support for a parochial benefice according to the listing in canon 1410. To insure a stable source of income, the law specifies that the contributions be certain and obligatory; otherwise there would be the risk of delayed or even defaulted payments. A sufficiently obligatory payment is one which the Church can demand in consequence of some juridic title, e.g., by reason of a bequest, by a claim in law, or through the prerogation of legal prescription.[43] Canon 1410 further specifies that only payments from families or moral persons may be constituted as an endowment. The obligatory payments of private individuals are not accepted as adequate, for ordinarily there will be no successor who at the demise of the donor will fall heir to the obligation of continuing them. Payments to be made by moral persons, on the other hand, certainly satisfy the demand for a stable source of income. Such would be the remunerations made to a pastor by a religious community to which a parish had been united. Governmental subsidies to clerics would also fall under this classification.[44]

The certain and voluntary offerings of the faithful constitute a third source of parochial revenue. They may be defined as movable goods which the faithful donate especially on the occasion of sacred functions for the use of the parish and its ministers.[45] The practice of making free-will offerings traces its origin back to the times of the Apostles. There were no laws regulating the matter, and yet the first Christians felt that they had a moral obligation to supply at least the necessaries of livelihood to the clergy and the poor. It was this custom that led to the introduction of the ancient system of offering tithes and first-fruits for the maintenance of the church and its ministers. Finally, in 1215 the IV General Council of the Lateran issued specific and replete instructions in relation to these offerings.[46] But custom again gradually supplanted the practice of contributing tithes and first-

---

[43] Cappello, *Summa Iuris Canonici,* II, 510-511.

[44] Blat, *Commentarium Textus Codicis Iuris Canonici* (5 vols. in 6, Romae, Collegio Angelico, 1919-1927; [Vols. II et III, 2. ed., Partes II-VI, 1921-1924]), III, Pars V, n. 305; cf. Ferreres, *Institutiones Canonicae,* II, 164.

[45] De Meester, *Compendium Juris Canonici,* III, 380.

[46] Cc. 32, 33, 35, X, *de decimis, primitiis et oblationibus,* III, 30.

fruits, so that now parishes depending upon this system for their support are a rarity.[47]

The methods of church support in the United States are varied and many.[48] Practically all, however, consist in the voluntary offerings of the faithful in one form or another. These offerings are recognized in law as constituting the endowment as it is defined in canon 1410. Some question could be raised regarding the validity of this classification, since a primary requirement of an endowment is that it possess the qualities of stability and perpetuity.[49] Are the free will offerings of the faithful sufficiently reliable and certain to warrant their establishment as an endowment?

It is true that in this country the faithful are not compelled to contribute to the support of the Church and the clergy,[50] but their traditional sense of duty in this matter is such that they feel, as did the early Christians, that they have a moral obligation to contribute what is necessary. They do not look upon their offerings as purely gratuitous, but rather as the fulfillment of a duty. Moreover, prior to the erection of a parish the financial habits of the prospec-

---

[47] The system of tithes is found in a few places in the United States (Des Moines, Iowa; Elkhart, Indiana); and a somewhat altered version of it in Seattle, Washington. See Connolly, *The Canonical Erection of Parishes,* p. 81, footnote n. 75.

[48] Kremer (*Church Support in the United States,* p. 68) offers this division: 1. Support from endowments. 2. Quasi-compulsory methods: assessments, pew rents, seat money collections, door collections. 3. Purely voluntary methods: offertory collections, free will donations, legacies. 4. Extraordinary methods: Bazaars, raffles, bingoes, etc.

[49] Coronata cites one author who acknowledges the certain and voluntary offerings of the faithful as an endowment in only such a case as the following one. A specific group of people, desiring to erect a parish, approach the ordinary and voluntarily oblige themselves to contribute a determined amount to the support of the parish. Coronata remarks that in this instance the offerings are voluntary and that they are certain at the same time, but he does not think that this is absolutely necessary. *Institutiones Iuris Canonici,* II, 361, footnote n. 3.

[50] Although the Church has the right to exact a sufficient means of support from the faithful (canon 1496), it has not enacted any universal law which compels the faithful to contribute. Perhaps the closest to which the Church has approached the exercise of its right to exact a sufficient means of support is found in canon 1502, in which it is stated that those things which pertain to the payment of first-fruits and tithes are to be regulated according to the special statutes and laudable customs of particular regions.

tive parishioners are sufficiently investigated to establish certitude concerning this source of income. It is on the basis of these things that free-will offerings can safely be described as adequately meeting the requirements of stability and perpetuity.

Prior to the Code there was some question whether stole fees could be established as a part of the endowment of a parish. Wernz (1842-1914) stated that, since they were necessarily offered for the sustentation of a pastor by force of ecclesiastical law, and were contributed not simply as a spontaneously given honorarium, they could correctly be considered as an endowment.[51] The Sacred Congregation of the Council, however, had previously implied that, since the amount from this source of income could not be determined beforehand, they were not to be admitted as an endowment for a benefice.[52] Canon 1410 now no longer leaves any doubt about the matter. It mentions stole fees as a possible endowment on an equal basis with property, invested capital, etc.

However, it must be noted that a positive declaration of the local ordinary is required before stole fees can be established as beneficial revenue. They cannot automatically be identified as a portion of the parochial patrimony.[53] On the contrary, they ordinarily form a part of the personal income of the pastor himself. Canon 463, § 1, grants the pastor the right to these fees. The power accorded to the ordinary through canons 1410 and 1414, § 2, to constitute them as parochial revenue implies in its use a derogation from the norms of canon 463, and so much be looked upon as an exception. Hence the pastor's rights to the stole fees must not be taken away unless the ordinary has a correspondingly good reason.[54]

---

[51] *Ius Decretalium,* III, n. 183.

[52] S. C. C., *Sabinen.,* 27 iun. 1807—*Thes. Resol.,* LXXIII (1807), 130.

[53] Sipos, *Enchiridion Iuris Canonici,* p. 726; Vermeersch-Creusen, *Epitome Iuris Canonici,* II, 524.

[54] As a matter of fact rarely does the ordinary avail himself of the power granted him through canons 1410 and 1414, § 2. In most of the dioceses of the United States the bishops have not found it necessary to claim that prerogative.

In no parishes of Spain do stole fees form a part of the endowment. They are considered as a means of support for the pastor, and his right to them may even be vindicated in the civil tribunals. Cf. Regatillo, *Institutiones Iuris Canonici* (2 vols., Vol. I, 2. ed., Satander: Sal· Terrae, 1946), I, 164.

The choir distributions, mentioned in canon 1410 as a possible beneficial endowment, find no application in the United States. Likewise, the means of obtaining an endowment for a parish as described in canon 1427, § 3, is of a very limited application in this country. By virtue of this canon the ordinary is empowered to assess a mother church in order to make up an endowment for a filial church. He is, however, denied the use of that power if it is possible to obtain the necessary revenue for the filial church through any of the means listed in canon 1410.[55]

---

[55] Connolly, *The Canonical Erection of Parishes,* p. 86.

CHAPTER VIII

The Competent Authority for the Erecting of Parishes

ARTICLE 1. THE METHODS OF THE ERECTION OF PARISHES

A discussion of the authorities competent for the erecting of parishes necessitates a preliminary consideration of the modes of erecting them, for the varying methods of establishing new parishes have a definite bearing upon this competency of the authorities.

Actually there are only three ways of erecting new parishes—by creation, by division, and by one form of extinctive union.

Erection of parishes by creation takes place when a previously undivided diocese or portion of a diocese is for the first time given territorial subdivisions according to the prescriptions of canon 216, § 1, so that new parishes come into existence where none had existed before. Since it is extremely rare to find in these days a diocese in which any portion of the territory and of the people has not been assigned to an already constituted parish, this means of erecting territorial parishes is practically non-existent, save in missionary regions.[1]

Erection of parishes by creation for particular groups whose individuality is established on a language or other personal basis is, however, not so uncommon. Until very recent times the influx of immigrants to many dioceses of this country necessitated the establishment of national parishes for them where none had existed before. Even now, because of increasing immigration quotas, it is not impossible to imagine circumstances in which the creation of new national parishes could be called for.

---

[1] Perhaps the only example of the creation of territorial parishes in a fully canonical diocese of comparatively modern times is the realignment of parishes that took place in France in 1801. Pope Pius VII (1800-1823) by concordat with the civil authorities in that year suppressed the existing parishes, and through this particular method established new ones. Cf. De Meester, *Compendium Juris Canonici,* III, 328.

The erection of parishes by way of division takes place when one or more new parishes are established in territory that pertained to one or several previously existing parishes.[2] This method is applicable in the constitution of new territorial parishes and in the founding of new national parishes (which ordinarily are of a mixed character, i.e., both territorial and personal.)[3]

A union of parishes is of an extinctive character when out of two or more suppressed parishes a new single parish is constituted, or when two or more parishes are united in such manner that at least one of the parishes ceases to exist.[4] An entirely new and distinct juridic entity is the direct result of the first form of extinctive union, but there is no constitution of a new moral person in the second form. In a consideration of the erection of parishes, it is only the first form that merits attention.

ARTICLE 2. THE VARIOUS AUTHORITIES CAPABLE OF ERECTING PARISHES

Emphasized throughout the historical synopsis of this work was the general necessity of the local ordinary's permission for the erection of a parish. Since in the normal course of events it is he to whom the establishment of parishes pertains, exclusive consideration was given to the part he played in the historical development of the parochial institute. The competency to erect parishes, however, is not limited to him alone. The Sovereign Pontiff, by virtue of his plenitude of power, can erect benefices of any sort in any part of the world without restriction relative to the manner in which they are erected. Under his authority the parish may come into existence by creation, by division or by extinctive union.

In the present Code the general authority to erect non-consistorial benefices in his own territory connotes competence for the

---

[2] Canon 1421.

[3] Division of parishes is not to be confused with dismemberment. Dismemberment occurs when a part of the territory or goods of one parish is taken away and assigned to another parish with no new moral person resulting.—Canon 1421. Cf. De Meester (*Compendium Juris Canonici,* III. 328) who fails to use the terms in their correct connotation.

[4] Canon 1419, § 1.

local ordinary to erect parishes.[5] The term "local ordinary" includes the residential bishop, abbots and prelates nullius, and their vicars general, administrators, vicars and prefects apostolic, and those who succeed them in rule.[6] The vicar general, however, is excluded in relation to the erection of benefices.[7]

The competency of the local ordinary is, of course, a more restricted one than that of the Roman Pontiff, and it varies with the kind of parish and the manner in which it becomes erected.

1. *Creation.* No restriction is placed by the general law upon the authority of the local ordinary with relation to the creation of territorial parishes.[8] His power is limited, however, in regard to the creation of personal or mixed parishes. "Personal or family parishes based on the diversity of language or citizenship of the faithful living in the same city or territory, cannot (*non possunt*) be constituted without an apostolic indult."[9] Permission of the Holy See is needed in each and every instance. There is some discussion whether the possession of an apostolic indult by the local ordinary is a condition that affects simply the lawfulness or also the validity of the act of erecting such parishes. The force of the words "*non possunt*" is not clear. They have long been an object of dispute among canonists.[10] The present writer feels that they have an invalidating effect, but whether they bespeak simply unlawfulness or also invalidity for a contrary act in this particular instance is seemingly an insoluble doubt. Since an invalidating law has no binding force when the very import of the law remains in doubt,[11] it must be asserted that a national or personal parish which is erected for a just cause may be considered validly, but not licitly, erected if the permission of the Holy See has not been obtained according to the prescript of canon 216, § 4.

The union of a parish with a religious house in full right and

[5] Canon 1414, § 2.
[6] Canon 198, § 2.
[7] Canon 1414, § 3.
[8] Canon 216, § 1.
[9] Canon 216, § 4.
[10] Cf. Ciesluk, *National Parishes*, pp. 81-84.
[11] Canon 15.

title (*pleno iure*) (which results in the creation of a religious parish), also the partial union, namely in temporals only, and even the conferral of a secular benefice upon a religious likewise cannot be accomplished by the local ordinary without an indult of the Holy See.[12]

2. *Division.* The ordinary, if he has a just and canonical cause, is empowered to divide any type of parish (*quaslibet paroecias*),[13] but with one exception. On his own authority he cannot divide a mixed or "national" parish. An apostolic indult is required for the division of this latter type of parish since division results in the constitution of a new mixed parish.[14] In relation to the division of exempt religious parishes, Augustine stated pertinently that, since an incorporated religious parish can be constituted only by the Holy See, it would seem presumptious for an ordinary to proceed to a division or dismemberment without informing the Holy See. He feels that this is a reasonable deduction since the boundaries of every religious parish are accepted and sanctioned by the Holy See.[15] However, since the Code does not require any such notification of the Apostolic See, the ordinary is certainly not bound to such action.

3. *Extinctive Union.* The erection of a parish by extinctive union is reserved to the Holy See.[16] No excusing circumstances are accepted as valid, mainly since a suppression of parishes is involved.

---

[12] Cons. 452, § 1; 1423, § 2; 1425, § 1; 1442.

[13] Canon 1427, § 1. Although canon 1427 places no restriction on the power of the vicar capitular (administrator) to divide parishes, some doubt has been raised as to his competency. Vermeersch-Creusen (*Epitome Iuris Canonici,* II, 532), as do most canonists, deny the power of the vicar capitular "on account of the analogy drawn from canon 1423" (according to which he is forbidden to unite parishes.) Connolly (*The Canonical Erection of Parishes,* pp. 49-50) holds the opposite view but wisely concludes: "In view of the negative opinion of most canonists it would seem unwise for the vicar capitular or administrator to proceed to a new foundation, unless the needs of the people are too urgent to brook delay. But if the vicar capitular or administrator establishes a new parish when all other conditions are verified, the division might be upheld by the Sacred Congregation of the Council."

[14] Canon 216, § 4.

[15] *A Commentary on the New Code of Canon Law,* VI, 509.

[16] Canon 1422.

ARTICLE 3. THE DECREE OF THE ERECTION OF PARISHES

The necessity of the intervention of ecclesiastical authority in the erection of parishes under the earlier law has been established with certitude. There likewise cannot be any doubt of its necessity under the present Code. In syllogistic form the argument is simple: No canonical moral person can obtain existence except through ecclesiastical authority.[17] A parish is a canonical moral person. Therefore absolutely essential to the existence of a parish is ecclesiastical authority.

While there can be no question that an intervening approbation of ecclesiastical authority is necessary in the erection of a parish, there has been much discussion regarding the manner in which that approbation is to be obtained. Moral personality can be conferred in two possible manners: either by the prescription of the law itself, or by the special concession of a competent ecclesiastical authority granted through a formal decree.[18] Is a formal decree of erection necessary for the valid constitution of a parish as a canonical moral person? Or may a parish obtain its personality through the prescription of the law itself?

Canon 1418 seems to demand a formal decree. A parish is a benefice, and that canon requires that "the erection of benefices is to be effected through a legal document in which the place where the benefice is erected is defined and in which the endowment of the benefice and the rights and obligations of the beneficiary are described." The Sacred Congregation of the Consistory in a declaration of August 1, 1919, likewise seemed to demand a formal decree as the sole means of erecting a parish.[19]

On the other hand, Canon 216 leaves the impression that a parish obtains its juridic personality through the prescription of the law itself. Paragraph 1 of that canon lists the elements ordinarily found in the constitution of a parish. A formal decree of erection is not included among them, and yet paragraph 3 of

[17] Brown, *The Canonical Juristic Personality with Special Reference to its Status in the United States of America,* The Catholic University of America Canon Law Studies, n. 39 (Washington, D. C.: The Catholic University of America, 1927), p. 91.

[18] Canon 100, § 1.

[19] *AAS,* XI (1919), 346.

the same canon states that with the verification of the elements mentioned in paragraph 1 the group is recognized as a parish. Moreover, in a response to the Apostolic Delegate of the United States (Sept. 26, 1921), Cardinal Gasparri, the chairman of the Pontifical Commission for the Authentic Interpretation of the Code, explicitly stated that a formal decree was not necessary for the erection of a parish, but that it was sufficient that the ordinary define territorial limits and assign a pastor to a church and to a group of the faithful which were within the determined limits.[20]

Thus was presented a problem to which there seemed to be no solution. However, a detailed examination of the canons and decrees led the Sacred Congregation of the Council to declare that a parish may be constituted in both ways—through prescription of the law itself as well as through a formal decree of erection. It stated that the legal document demanded in canon 1418 ("which properly taken is not the same thing as a formal decree of erection") was required only by precept, not, however, for the valid constitution of a benefice. The same, it added, must be held concerning the decree which was required by the Sacred Congregation of the Consistory in its declaration of August 1, 1919.[21]

The matter is therefore beyond all question: a formal decree is not necessary for the valid constitution of a parish. But the element of lawfulness postulates its presence. It is true that the requirement relative to the element of lawfulness cannot be proved conclusively from canon 1418, for the legal document referred to in this canon, as has been said, simply serves as proof of the canonical erection; it is not the decree of erection itself, for that consists simply in the act of the bishop.[22] Still the already cited declaration of the Sacred Congregation of the Consistory of August 1, 1919, cannot be mistaken. It definitely does require a formal decree as a condition of lawfulness for the erection of benefices. One cannot rightfully object that the response

[20] Bouscaren, *Digest,* I, 149.

[21] *Principis Alberten. et Saskatoonen.,* 5 mart. 1932—*AAS,* XXV (1933), 437.

[22] Maroto, "Animadversiones in Decretum S.C.C., *Principis Alberten et Saskatoonen,* 5 mart. 1932," *Apollinaris* (Romae, 1928—), VI (1933), 425-426; cf. Connolly, *The Canonical Erection of Parishes,* p. 72.

of Cardinal Gasparri, referred to above, seems to indicate the contrary. His reply concerned exclusively the element of validity in the constituting of a parish, and not also the matter of lawfulness.

Hence in normal circumstances the ordinary is certainly obliged to erect a parish by means of a formal decree. The decree itself could possibly be given in an oral manner, but ordinarily it should be in writing.[23] If it is oral, then as a matter of lawfulness it is still demanded that proof of the act be established by means of a legal document in accord with the prescription of canon 1418. If it is in writing, then the decree of erection should also accord with the rule expressed in the same canon. In this latter instance the formal decree and the legal document that is mentioned in canon 1418 are identical. In the prior instance they are of course distinct, but in practice amount to the same thing. In applying the prescript of canon 1418 with reference to the erection of a parish, the Sacred Congregation of the Consistory declared that the legal document should define the territorial limits of the parish, describe the site of the parish, declare what the sources of revenue will be, and finally express whether the appointed pastor is to be classed among the removable or the irremovable pastors in the diocese.[24]

A similar instruction was issued for mission territory by the Sacred Congregation for the Propagation of the Faith. "The erection of a quasi-parish is to be effected by means of a decree of the ordinary, which shall clearly define the boundaries of the territory, or, if this is impossible, at least state the principal Christian settlements which belong to it, and also designate the principal church and the residence of the quasi-pastor."[25]

---

[23] "CAUSA seu *auctor* personalitatem dans, est . . . Ecclesia . . . sive *a iure* . . . vel *per formale decretum* competentis superioris (c. 100, § 1), v.c. hospitale. *Formale* est quod implicite vel explicite exprimat naturam collegii vel instituti et personalitatis concessionem; ad valorem non requiritur scriptum, sed expedit."—Regatillo, *Institutiones Iuris Canonici,* I, 130.

If the decree is oral, it would necessarily have to be given in a public session or before at least two witnesses; otherwise it could not be described as "formal."

[24] 1 aug. 1919—*AAS,* XI (1919), 346.

[25] 25 iul. 1920—*AAS,* XII (1920), 331.

A sample document for the erection of parishes follows:

Formula erectionis novae paroeciae[26]

Nos. N. N., gratia Dei et auctoritate Apostolicae Sedis Episcopus N., omnibus praesentes litteras inspecturis salutem et in Domino benedictionem.

Inter praecipua Nostri pastoralis officii munera sane habetur commoda divini cultus pro omnibus singulisque fidelibus Nostrae curae commissis ita disponi ut unusquisque parochus cunctis officii per Nos ei attributi numeribus facilius satisfacere possit et valeat. Idcirco, prius auditis parochis incolisque paroeciarum . . . et Decano N. . . . et omnibus quorum interest, necnon etiam super tam grave negotium requisita Capituli Nostri Cathedralis (Consultorum Dioecesanorum) sententia per votum regulariter emissum, novam paroeciam ad divini cultus necessitatibus et religionis incremento plenius providendum canonice erigi decrevimus.

Quae quidem paroecia consistat intra limites infra dictos, scilicet:[27] ______________________ cum ecclesia paroeciali in loco N. . . . existente, et ad decanatum N. . . . spectet.

Nova paroecia erit inamovibilis (vel amovibilis) iuxta can. 454, § 3.

Dos beneficii parochialis in his temporalibus habeatur bonis, scilicet:[28] ______________________________

Iura vero ac onera parochi pro tempore beneficiarii, praeter ea ex iure communi sunt et erunt, nempe:[29] __________________

[26] Taken from Connolly, *The Canonical Erection of Parishes*, p. 113.

[27] Here should be described carefully, clearly, and in detail, the limits of the parochial territory for the purpose of effectively forestalling future uncertainty and litigation.

[28] Here should be listed the temporal goods, movable and immovable, that constitute the endowment of the benefice. If this endowment cannot be determined, the local ordinary ought, in conformity with canon 1415, § 3, to declare at least in a summary fashion, yet as definitely as possible, what source of income will provide for the expenses of worship in the parish and for the adequate livelihood of the sacred ministers.

[29] Here should be indicated the special obligations attached to the benefice in virtue of the foundation. If there are none, the paragraph should be replaced with the following: *Iura vero ac onera parochi pro tempore beneficarii sunt ea dumtaxat ex iure communi praescripta.*

Quapropter, omnibus iuxta canones attente consideratis et mature perpensis, hanc dictam paroeciam N . . . ut supra descriptam, cum praefata ecclesia paroeciali in loco . . . sub titulo S . . . virtute praesentium canonice erigimus erectamque declaramus; cum omnibus iuribus, gratiis et facultatibus et fabricae consilio, quibus ceterae Nostrae dioecesis paroeciae, tam in spiritualibus quam in temporalibus, iuxta canones et statuta dioecesana frui et gaudere solent. In nomine Patris et Filii et Spiritus Sancti. Amen.

Datum N., sub signo sigilloque Nostris, ac cancellarii Nostri subscriptione, anno Domini millesimo nongentesimo . . . die . . . mensis. . . .

Loc. + sigil. N.N. Episcopus N.

N.N. Cancellarius.

CONCLUSIONS

Parishes and quasi-parishes are essentially identical, differing only because of the different kind of hierarchical unit of which they form a part. Hence legislation which applies to the parish is with but few exceptions equally applicable to the quasi-parish.

The constitutive elements of parishes (also of quasi-parishes) are six in number. Three elements are inherently essential in the constitution of every type of parish: a determinate group of the faithful, the office of pastor, and the act of a competent ecclesiastical authority erecting the parish. Three elements may be described as "accessory"—usually present but not necessarily so: territorial limits, a church building and an adequate endowment.

1. Territorial Limits

a) Although of an absolutely essential character in the constitution of a territorial parish, territorial limits are of a merely accessory character in the generic definition of a parish.

b) The Church has from the earliest times shown a preference for a territorial grouping of the faithful of a diocese, and still in the present law recognizes it as the most convenient form for partitioning the diocese into parishes.

c) A precise description of the boundaries of territorial parishes must be found in every case. The Ordinary cannot, as a general rule, simply decree that the halfway line between two given parochial churches constitutes the parochial demarcation of territory for the two neighboring parishes.

d) The norm of Canon 1509, 4°, which declares the fixed and certain territorial limits of parishes not to be subject to the agency of legal prescription, is to be extended also to the boundaries of quasi-parishes if they are equally fixed and certain.

e) While allowing the national parish to retain its original status in relation to all its members who are of a particular nationality, the Ordinary may assign to the national parish fixed territorial boundaries within the limits of which the national pastor may exercise jurisdiction also over the general populace. Such action necessitates an apostolic indult.

2. Determinate Group of the Faithful.

a) Since his flock is sufficiently determinate, and inasmuch as all other requirements are present, a United States military chaplain must be looked upon as a personal pastor.

b) The erection of parishes for Catholics of any oriental rite does not fall under the restrictive prescription of canon 216, § 4. No apostolic indult is required for the erection or the modification of such parishes.

c) Negro parishes are ordinarily personal parishes. Unless they are erected in a district solidly or almost solidly inhabited by negroes, and the pastor is given jurisdiction over the general populace of the district, an apostolic indult is needed for their erection.

d) A minimum of ten families is required for the licit erection of a parish.

3. The Office of Pastor.

a) The office of pastor, and not the actual incumbency of a pastor, must be listed among the absolutely essential elements of a parish.

b) Indications of the parochial status of a church may be derived from a consideration of the rector's rights and obligations: his right to baptize; his power to assist at matrimony; his obligation to apply the *missa pro populo;* his right to conduct funeral services and to distribute paschal Communion. If all these signs are present, the rector is most likely a true pastor, and his church a true parish church. If one or the other sign is lacking, the contrary cannot be affirmed immediately.

c) Parochial vicars and assistant pastors in charge of mission stations are distinguished from pastors by the fact that they have been granted their charges simply as administrational functions (*in administrationem*), and not as vested claims (*in titulum*).

4. The Church Building.

a) A parish may be established before the construction of a church building.

b) In the establishment of a parish, however, there must always be present the intention to erect a church building.

5. Adequate Endowment.

a) While a parish may be erected without an adequate endowment, yet it is required by law that there be present at least some minute, though insufficient, measure of endowment.

b) A parochial benefice may lose its endowment completely and still continue in existence as a parochial benefice.

6. The Act of the Competent Ecclesiastical Authority for the Erecting of the Parish.

a) A parish may come into existence through a formal decree of erection executed by a competent ecclesiastical authority, but the formal decree is not necessary in and of itself. Although the formal decree is necessary as a condition for lawfulness, a church may also gain parochial status through the enabling prescription of the law.

b) The formal decree of erection is not necessarily identical with the legal document called for in canon 1418.

c) The formal decree of itself need not necessarily be a written document, but proof of the formal decree in writing is required by the law.

BIBLIOGRAPHY

Sources

Acta Apostolicae Sedis, Commentarium Officiale, Romae, 1909—

Acta et Decreta, Concilii Plenarii Baltimorensis Tertii A. D. MDCCCLXXXIV, Baltimorae: John Murphy, 1886.

Acta Sanctae Sedis, 41 vols., Romae, 1865-1908.

Bouscaren, T. Lincoln, *The Canon Law Digest,* 2 vols., Milwaukee: Bruce, 1934, 1943.

Bullarum, Diplomatum et Privilegiorum Sanctorum Pontificum Taurinensis Editio, 24 vols. et Appendix, Augustae Taurinorum, 1857-1872.

Canones et Decreta Sacrosancti Oecumenici Concilii Tridentini, Editio novissima ad fidem Optimorum exemplarium Castigate impressa (XIX reimpressio stereotypa), Taurini, 1913.

Codex Iuris Canonici Pii X Pontificis Maximi iussi digestus Benedicti Papae XV auctoritate promulgatus, praefatione fontium annotatione et indice analytico-alphabetico ab Eño Petro Card. Gasparri auctus, Romae: Typis Vaticanis, 1917; Reimpressio: Westminster, Maryland: The Newman Book Shop, 1946.

Codicis Iuris Canonici Fontes, cura Eñi Petri Card. Gasparri editi, 9 vols., Romae (postea Civitate Vaticana): Typis Polyglottis Vaticanis, 1923-1939 (Vols. VII, VIII, IX, ed. cura et studio Eñi Iustiniani Card. Serédi).

Collectanea S. Congregationis de Propaganda Fide, 2 vols., Romae: Typographia Polyglotta, S.C. de Propaganda Fide, 1907.

Concilii Plenarii Baltimorensis II Acta et Decreta, Baltimorae: Joannes Murphy et Soc., 1868.

Corpus Iuris Canonici, ed. Lipsiensis 2. post Aemilii Ludovici Richteri curas . . . instruxit Aemilius Friedberg, 2 vols., Lipsiae: Tauchnitz, 1879-1881; ed. anatastice repetita, 1928.

Decretales D. Gregorii Papae IX, suae integritati, una cum glossis restitutae, Romae, 1582.

Decretum Gratiani, emendatum et notationibus illustratum, una cum glossis, 2 vols., Romae, 1582.

Hardouin, Jean, *Acta Conciliorum et Epistolae Decretales ac Constitutiones Summorum Pontificum,* 12 vols., Parisiis, 1714-1715.

Hinschius, Paulus, *Decretales Pseudo-Isidorianae et Capitula Agilramni,* Lipsiae, 1863.

Jaffé, Phillipus, *Regesta Pontificum Romanorum ab condita Ecclesia ad annum post Christum natum MCXCVIII,* 2. ed., correctam et auctam auspiciis Gulielmi Wattenbach curaverunt K. Kaltenbrunner, P. Ewald, Löwenfeld, 2 vols., Lipsiae, 1885-1888.

Mansi, J. D., *Sacrorum Conciliorum Nova et Amplissima Collectio,* 53 vols. in 60, Parisiis, 1901-1927.

Monumenta Germaniae Historica, 188 vols., incomplete, Hannoverae, 1826—; *Leges in 4,* Sectio II (*Capitularia Regum Francorum*), T. I, ed. A. Boretius, 1883; T. II, ed. A. Boretius et V. Krause, 1897; Sectio III (*Concilia*), T. I, ed. F. Maassen, 1893.

Pallotini, S., *Collectio omnium conclusionum et resolutionum quae in causis propositis apud Sacram Congregationem Cardinalium S. Concilii Tridentini Interpretum prodierunt ab eius institutione anno MDLXIV ad annum MDCCCLX, distinctis titulis alphabetico ordine per materias digesta,* 18 vols., Romae, 1868-1895.

Potthast, A., *Regesta Pontificum Romanorum inde ab anno post Christum natum MCXCVIII ad annum MCCCIV,* 2 vols., Berolini, 1874-1875.

Sacrae Romanae Rotae Decisiones seu Sententiae (ab anno 1909—), Romae: Typis Vaticanis, 1912—.

Sacrae Rotae Romanae Decisiones Recentiores, Part. I,Francofurti, 1623.

Thesaurus Resolutionum Sacrae Congregationis Concilii, 167 vols., Romae, 1718-1908.

Authors

Augustine, Charles, *A Commentary on the New Code of Canon Law,* 8 vols., Vol. II, 3. ed., St. Louis: Herder and Co., 1919.

Ayrinhac, H. A., *The Administrative Legislation in the New Code of Canon Law,* New York: Longmans, Green and Co., 1930.

Badii, Caesar, *Institutiones Iuris Canonici,* 3. ed., 2 vols., Florentiae, 1921.

Barbosa, Augustinus, *Iuris Ecclesiastici Universi Libri Tres,* Lugduni, 1660.

———, *De Officio et Potestate Parochi,* Animadversiones et addimenta Ubaldi Giraldi, Romae, 1831.

Bernier, Paulus, *De Patrimonio Paroeciali,* Quebeci: apud Auctorem, 2, via Port Dauphin, 1938.

Beste, U., *Introductio in Codicem,* 2. ed., Collegeville, Minnesota: St. John's Abbey Press, 1944.

Blat, Albertus, *Commentarium Textus Codicis Iuris Canonici,* 5 vols. in 6, Romae: Collegio Angelico, 1919-1927; Vols. II et III, Partes II-VI, 2. ed., 1921-1924.

Boehmer, I. H., *Jus Parochiale,* Halae, 1760.

Bouix, D., *Tractatus de Parocho,* 3. ed., Parisiis, 1880.

Bouscaren, T.-Ellis, A., *Canon Law, A Text and Commentary,* Milwaukee: Bruce, 1946.

Brown, Brendan F., *The Canonical Juristic Personality with Special Reference to its Status in the United States of America,* The Catholic University of America Canon Law Studies, n. 38, Washington, D. C.: The Catholic University of America, 1927.

Cappello, F. M., *Summa Iuris Canonici,* 3 vols., Vols. I, II, 4. ed., 1945; Vol. III, 3. ed., 1940, Romae: Universitas Gregoriana.

———, *Tractatus Canonico-moralis de Sacramentis,* 3 vols. in 6, Vol. I, 4. ed., Romae: Marietti, 1945.

Cavanaugh, William T., *The Reservation of the Blessed Sacrament,* The Catholic University of America Canon Law Studies, n. 40, Washington, D. C.: The Catholic University of America, 1927.

Chelodi, Joannes, *Ius de Personis,* 3. ed., cura P. Ciprotti, Vicenza: Societá Anonima Tipografia, 1942.

Ciesluk, Joseph E., *National Parishes in the United States,* The Catholic University of America Canon Law Studies, n. 190, Washington, D. C.: The Catholic University of America Press, 1944.

Claeys Bouuaert,-Simenon, G., *Manuale Juris Canonici,* 3 vols., Vols. I et III, 4. ed., Gandae et Leodii: Dessain, 1934.

Cocchi, Guidus, *Commentarium in Codicem Iuris Canonici,* 8 vols., Taurinorum Augustae: Marietti, 1931-1940. Vol. III, 4. ed., 1940.

Connolly, Nicholas P., *The Canonical Erection of Parishes,* The Catholic University of America Canon Law Studies, n. 114, Washington, D. C.: The Catholic University of America, 1938.

Coronata, Mattaeus Conte a, *Institutiones Iuris Canonici,* 2. ed., 5 vols., Taurini: Marietti, 1936-1947.

De Angelis, Phillipus, *Praelectiones Iuris Canonici,* 5 vols., Romae, 1908.

De Luca, Ioannes Card., *Theatrum Veritatis et Iustitiae,* 16 vols., Coloniae Agrippinae, 1706.

De Meester, A., *Juris Canonici et Juris Canonico-Civilis Compendium,* nova editio, 4 vols., Brugis, 1921-1928.

Du Cange, Carolus Dufresne, *Glossarium ad Scriptores Mediae et Infimae Latinitatis,* 6 vols., Parisiis, 1733.

Duchesne, Louis, Le LIBER PONTIFICALIS, *Texte, Introduction et Commentaire,* 2 vols., Parisiis, 1886-1892.

Fagnanus, Prosper, *Commentaria in Quinque Libros Decretalium,* 4 vols., Venetiis, 1697.

Fanfani, Ludovicus, *De Iure Parochorum ad Norman Codicis Iuris Canonici,* Romae, 1924.

Ferraris, Lucius, *Prompta Bibliotheca Canonica, Iuridica, Moralis, Theologica, necnon Ascetica, Polemica, Rubricistica, Historica,* ed. noviss., 9 vols., Romae, 1885-1899.

Ferreres, Joannes P., *Institutiones Canonicae,* ed. altera, 2 vols., Barcinone, 1920.

Fournier, P.-LeBras, G., *Histoire des Collections Canoniques en Occident depuis les Fausses Décrétales jusqu' au Décret de Gratien,* 2 vols., Paris, Recueil Sirey, 1931-1932.

Golden, Henry F., *Parochial Benefices in the New Code,* The Catholic University of America Canon Law Studies, n. 10, Washington, D. C.: The Catholic University of America, 1925.

Gonzales-Tellez, Manuel, *Commentaria in Quinque Libros Decretalium,* 5 vols. in 4, Venetiis, 1699.

Hostiensis, Cardinalis (Henricus de Segusia), *Summa Aurea,* Venetiis, 1570.

Houwen, Victorinus, *De Parochorum Statu,* Dissertatio Historico-Canonica, Lovanii, 1848.

Kelly, Bernard M., *The Functions Reserved to Pastors,* The Catholic University of America Canon Law Studies, n. 250, Washington, D. C.: The Catholic University of America Press, 1947.

Kremer, Michael N., *Church Support in the United States,* The Catholic University of America Canon Law Studies, n. 61, Washington, D. C.: The Catholic University of America, 1930.

Leage, R. W., *Roman Private Law,* 2. ed. by C. H. Ziegler, London: Macmillan, 1932.

Kurtscheid, *Historia Juris Canonici, Historia Institutionum,* Vol. I (ab Ecclesiae Fundatione usque ad Gratianum), Romae: Officium Libri Catholici, 1941.

Leurenius, Petrus, *Forum Beneficiale,* 2 vols., Venetiis, 1752.

Maroto, Phillipus, *Institutiones Iuris Canonici,* 2 vols., Matriti, 1918-1919.

Maupied, Franciscus, *Juris Canonici Universi Compendium,* 2 vols., ed. J. P. Migne, Parisiis, 1863.

Migne, J. P., *Patrologiae Cursus Completus, Series Latina,* 221 vols., Parisiis, 1844-1864.

Mundy, Thomas M., *The Union of Parishes,* The Catholic University of America Canon Law Studies, n. 204, Washington, D. C.: The Catholic University of America Press, 1945.

Nicolaus de Tudeschis (Abbas Panormitanus), *Commentaria in Quinque Libros Decretalium,* 8 vols., Venetiis, 1588.

Pirhing, Ernricus, *Ius Canonicum in Quinque Libros Decretalium Distributum,* 5 vols. in 4, Dilingae, 1674-1678.

Pistocchi, Marius, *De Re Beneficiali,* Taurini, 1928.

Regatillo, E., *Institutiones Iuris Canonici,* 2 vols., Vol. I, 2. ed., Santander: Sal Terrae, 1946.

Reiffenstuel, Analectus, *Ius Canonicum Universum,* 5 vols. in 7, Venetiis, 1735.

Rossi, Ioannes, *De Paroecia,* Romae; Pustet, 1923.

Rufinus, *Die Summa Decretorum des Magister Rufinus,* ed. H. Singer, Paderborn, 1902.

Schaefer, T., *Pfarrkirche und Stift im deutschen Mittelalter,* Kirchenrechtliche Abhandlungen hrsg. von U. Stutz, 3. Heft, Stuttgart, 1903.

Schmalzgrueber, F., *Ius Ecclesiasticum Universum,* 5 vols. in 12, Romae, 1843-1845.

Sipos, S., *Enchiridion Iuris Canonici,* Pecs, 1926.

Smith, S. B., *Elements of Ecclesiastical Law,* 3 vols., Vol. I, 9. ed., New York, 1893.

Stutz, Ulrich, "The Proprietary Church as an Element of Mediaeval Germanic Ecclesiastical Law," *Studies in Medieval History, Mediaeval Germany (911-1252)*, translated by Geoffrey Barraclough, 2 vols., Oxford: Blackwell, 1938.

Thomassinus, Ludovicus, *Vetus et Nova Ecclesiae Disciplina,* 10 vols., Parisiis, 1688.

Tunzi, Pasquale, *Condizione giuridica della parrochia nel diritto canonico e nel diritto ecclesiastico italiano,* Romae: Univ. Gregoriana, 1938.

Van Espen, Bernardus, *Jus Ecclesiasticum Universum,* ed. novis., 10 vols. in 5, Venetiis, 1789.

Vermeersch, A.-Creusen, J., *Epitome Iuris Canonici,* 6. ed., 3 vols., Mechliniae: H. Dessain, 1937-1946.

Waldron, Joseph F., *The Minister of Baptism,* The Catholic University of America Canon Law Studies, n. 170, Washington, D. C.: The Catholic University of America Press, 1942.

Wernz, F. X., *Ius Decretalium,* 6 vols., Romae, 1898-1905.

Wernz, F. X.-Vidal, P., *Ius Canonicum,* 7 vols. in 8, Romae: Apud Aedes Universitatis Gregorianae, 1923-1938.

Woywod, Stanislaus, *A Practical Commentary on the Code of Canon Law,* 5 ed., 2 vols., New York: Joseph F. Wagner, 1939.

Articles

Bastnagel, Clement V., "Is a Parish for Colored People a 'National' Parish?" *ER,* CVIII (1943), 382-384.

Kaiser, R., "Ecclesiastical Legislation on the *Missa pro Populo,*" *ER,* LXI (1919), 369-371.

Maroto, Philippus, "Animadversiones in Decretum S.C. Concilii, Principis Alberten et Saskatoonen., 5 mart. 1932," *Apollinaris,* VI (1933), 423-431.

Studies and Conferences, "National and Canonical Parishes in the United States," *ER,* LXXVI (1927), 90-91.

Studies and Conferences, "National Pastors and Assistance at Marriage," *ER,* LXXX (1929), 89.

Studies and Conferences, "Pastor Halloft and Foreign Born Catholics," *ER,* LXXII (1925), 85.

Periodicals

American Ecclesiastical Review, The (from Vol. XXXIII, July, 1905-Vol. CIX, December, 1943. *The Ecclesiastical Review*), Philadelphia, 1889-1943; Baltimore, 1944—.

Analecta Ecclesiastica, Romae, 1893-1911.

Apollinaris, Romae, 1928—.

ABBREVIATIONS

AAS—*Acta Apostolicae Sedis.*
AER—*The American Ecclesiastical Review.*
ASS—*Acta Sanctae Sedis.*
Bull. Rom.—*Bullarum Diplomatum et Privilegiorum Sanctorum Pontificum Taurinensis Editio.*
ER—*The Ecclesiastical Review.*
Fontes—*Codicis Iuris Canonici Fontes cura . . . Gasparri editi.*
Hardouin—*Acta Conciliorum, etc.*
Jaffé—*Regesta Pontificum Romanorum.*
Mansi—*Sacrorum Conciliorum Nova et Amplissima Collectio.*
MGH—*Monumenta Germaniae Historica.*
MPL—*Migne, Patrologia Latina.*
Pont. Comm. ad Int. C.I.C.—Pontificia Commissio ad Codicem Iuris Canonici Authentice Interpretandum.
S.C.C.—Sacra Congregatio Concilii.
S.C. Consist.—Sacra Congregatio Consistorialis.
S.C. de Prop. Fide—Sacra Congregatio de Propaganda Fide.

BIOGRAPHICAL NOTE

Anthony B. Mickells was born on June 4, 1918, at Omaha, Nebraska. After attending Sts. Peter and Paul Parochial School in that city, in 1931 he began his studies for the Priesthood at St. Lawrence College, Mt. Calvary, Wisconsin, and continued his studies there for six years. After completing his course in Philosophy in 1939 at St. Louis Preparatary Seminary, he entered Kenrick Theological Seminary, St. Louis. He was ordained to the Holy Priesthood in May, 1943, and served in parish work for three years. In September, 1946, he enrolled in the School of Canon Law of the Catholic University of America, where he received the Degrees J.C.B. and J.C.L. in the years 1947 and 1948 respectively.

INDEX

CANON LAW STUDIES*

1. Freriks, Rev. Celestine A., C.PP.S., J.C.D., Religious Congregations in Their External Relations, 121 pp. 1916.
2. Galliher, Rev. Daniel M., O.P., J.C.D., Canonical Elections, 117 pp., 1917.
3. Borkowski, Rev. Aurelius L., O.F.M., J.C.D., De Confraternibus Ecclesiasticis, 136 pp., 1918.
4. Castillo, Rev. Cayo, J.C.D., Disertacion Historico-Canonica sobre la Potestad del Cabildo en Sede Vacante o Impedida del Vicario Capitular, 99 pp., 1919 (1918).
5. Kubelbeck, Rev. William J., S.T.B., J.C.D., The Sacred Penitentiaria and Its Relation to Faculties of Ordinaries and Priests, 129 pp., 1918.
6. Petrovits, Rev. Joseph, J.C., S.T.D., J.C.D., The New Church Law on Matrimony, X-461 pp., 1919.
7. Hickey, Rev. John J., S.T.B., J.C.D., Irregularities and Simple Impediments in the New Code of Canon Law, 100 pp., 1920.
8. Klekotka, Rev. Peter J., S.T.B., J.C.D., Diocesan Consultors, 179 pp., 1920.
9. Wanenmacher, Rev. Francis, J.C.D., The Evidence in Ecclesiastical Procedure Affecting the Marriage Bond, 1920 (Printed 1935).
10. Golden, Rev. Henry Francis, J.C.D., Parochial Benefices in the New Code, IV-119 pp., 1921 (Printed 1925).
11. Koudelka, Rev. Charles J., J.C.D., Pastors, Their Rights and Duties According to the New Code of Canon Law, 211 pp., 1921.
12. Melo, Rev. Antonius, O.F.M., J.C.D., De Exemptione Regularium, X-188 pp., 1921.
13. Schaaf, Rev. Valentine Theodore, O.F.M., S.T.B., J.C.D., The Cloister, X-180 pp., 1921.
14. Burke, Rev. Thomas Joseph, S.T.D., J.C.D., Competence in Ecclesiastical Tribunals, IV-117 pp., 1922.
15. Leech, Rev. George Leo, J.C.D., A Comparative Study of the Constitution "Apostolicae Sedis" and the "Codex Juris Canonici," 179 pp., 1922.
16. Motry, Rev. Hubert Louis, S.T.D., J.C.D., Diocesan Faculties According to the Code of Canon Law, II-167 pp., 1922.
17. Murphy, Rev. George Lawrence, J.C.D., Delinquencies and Penalties in the Administration and the Reception of the Sacraments, IV-121 pp., 1923.

*All published numbers are available from the Catholic University of America Press, 620 Michigan Avenue, N.E., Washington 17, D. C., except the following: Nos. 1-114 inclusive, 115, 118, 120, 122, 123, 136, 153, 162, 182 and 198. But the following numbers, now reissued, are obtainable from *The Jurist*, The Catholic University of America, Washington 17, D. C., namely: Nos. 5, 7, 11, 17, 18, 19, 26, 28, 30, 31, 34, 42, 44, 51, 52 and 61.

18. O'Reilly, Rev. John Anthony, S.T.B., J.C.D., Ecclesiastical Sepulture in the New Code of Canon Law, II-129 pp., 1923.
19. Michalicka, Rev. Wenceslas Cyrill, O.S.B., J.C.D., Judicial Procedure in Dismissal of Clerical Exempt Religious, 107 pp., 1923.
20. Dargin, Rev. Edward Vincent, S.T.B., J.C.D., Reserved Cases According to the Code of Canon Law, IV-103 pp., 1924.
21. Godfrey, Rev. John A., S.T.B., J.C.D., The Right of Patronage According to the Code of Canon Law, 153 pp., 1924.
22. Hagedorn, Rev. Francis Edward, J.C.D., General Legislation on Indulgences, II-154 pp., 1924.
23. King, Rev. James Ignatius, J.C.D., The Administration of the Sacraments to Dying Non-Catholics, V-141 pp., 1924.
24. Winslow, Rev. Francis Joseph, O.F.M., J.C.D., Vicars and Prefects Apostolic, IV-149 pp., 1924.
25. Correa, Rev. Jose Servelion, S.T.L., J.C.D., La Potestad Legislativa de la Iglesia Catolica, IV-127 pp., 1925.
26. Dugan, Rev. Henry Francis, A.M., J.C.D., The Judiciary Department of the Diocesan Curia, 87 pp., 1925.
27. Keller, Rev. Charles Frederick, S.T.B., J.C.D., Mass Stipends, 167 pp., 1925.
28. Paschang, Rev. John Linus, J.C.D., The Sacramentals According to the Code of Canon Law, 129 pp., 1925.
29. Piontek, Rev. Cyrillus, O.F.M., S.T.B., J.C.D., De Indulto Exclaustrationis necnon Saecularizationis, XIII-289 pp., 1925.
30. Kearney, Rev. Richard Joseph, S.T.B., J.C.D., Sponsors at Baptism According to the Code of Canon Law, IV-127 pp., 1925.
31. Bartlett, Rev. Chester Joseph, A.M., LL.B., J.C.D., The Tenure of Parochial Property in the United States of America, V-108 pp., 1926.
32. Kilker, Rev. Adrian Jerome, J.C.D., Extreme Unction, V-425 pp., 1926.
33. McCormick, Rev. Robert Emmett, J.C.D., Confessors of Religious, VIII-266 pp., 1926.
34. Miller, Rev. Newton Thomas, J.C.D., Founded Masses According to the Code of Canon Law, VII-93 pp., 1926.
35. Roelker, Rev. Edward G., S.T.D., J.C.D., Principles of Privilege According to the Code of Canon Law, XI-166 pp., 1926.
36. Bakalarczyk, Rev. Richardus, M.I.C., J.U.D., De Novitiatu, VIII-208 pp., 1927.
37. Pizzuti, Rev. Lawrence, O.F.M., J.U.L., De Parochis Religiosis, 1927. (Not Printed.)
38. Bliley, Rev. Nicholas Martin, O.S.B., J.C.D., Altars According to the Code of Canon Law, XIX-132 pp., 1927.
39. Brown, Mr. Brendan Francis, A.B., LL.M., J.U.D., The Canonical Juristic Personality with Special Reference to its Status in the United States of America, V-212 pp., 1927.

40. Cavanaugh, Rev. William Thomas, C.P., J.U.D., The Reservation of the Blessed Sacrament, VIII-101 pp., 1927.
41. Doheny, Rev. William J., C.S.C., A.B., J.C.D., Church Property: Modes of Acquisition, X-118 pp., 1927.
42. Feldhaus, Rev. Aloysius H., C.PP.S., J.C.D., Oratories, IV-141 pp., 1927.
43. Kelly, Rev. James Patrick, A.B., J.C.D., The Jurisdiction of the Simple Confessor, X-208 pp., 1927.
44. Neuberger, Rev. Nicholas J., J.C.D., Canon 6 or the Relation of the Codex Iuris Canonici to the Preceding Legislation, V-95 pp., 1927.
45. O'Keefe, Rev. Gerald Michael, J.C.D., Matrimonial Dispensations, Powers of Bishops, Priests, and Confessors, VIII-232 pp., 1927.
46. Quigley, Rev. Joseph A. M., A.B., J.C.D., Condemned Societies, 139 pp., 1927.
47. Zaplotnik, Rev. Johannes Leo, J.C.D., De Vicariis Foraneis, X-142 pp., 1927.
48. Duskie, Rev. John Aloysius, A.B., J.C.D., The Canonical Status of the Orientals in the United States, VIII-196 pp., 1928.
49. Hyland, Rev. Francis Edward, J.C.D., Excommunication, Its Nature, Historical Development and Effects, VIII-181 pp., 1928.
50. Reimann, Rev. Gerald Joseph, O.M.C., J.C.D., The Third Order Secular of Saint Francis, 201 pp., 1928.
51. Schenk, Rev. Francis J., J.C.D., The Matrimonial Impediments of Mixed Religion and Disparity of Cult, XVI-318 pp., 1929.
52. Coady, Rev. John Joseph, S.T.D., J.U.D., A.M., The Appointment of Pastors, VIII-150 pp., 1929.
53. Kay, Rev. Thomas Henry, J.C.D., Competence in Matrimonial Procedure, VIII-164 pp., 1929.
54. Turner, Rev. Sidney Joseph, C.P., J.U. D., The Vow of Poverty, XLIX-217 pp., 1929.
55. Kearney, Rev. Raymond A., A.B., S.T.D., J.C.D., The Principles of Delegation, VII-149 pp., 1929.
56. Conran, Rev. Edward James, A.B., J.C.D., The Interdict, V-163 pp., 1930.
57. O'Neill, Rev. William H., J.C.D., Papal Rescripts of Favor, VII-218 pp., 1930.
58. Bastnagel, Rev. Clement Vincent, J.U.D., The Appointment of Parochial Adjutants and Assistants, XV-257 pp., 1930.
59. Ferry, Rev. William A., A.B., J.C.D., Stole Fees, V-136 pp., 1930.
60. Costello, Rev. John Michael, A.B., J.C.D., Domicile and Quasi-Domicile, VII-201 pp., 1930.
61. Kremer, Rev. Michael Nicholas, A.B., S.T.B., J.C.D., Church Support in the United States, VI-136 pp., 1930.
62. Angulo, Rev. Luis, C.M., J.C.D., Legislation de la Iglesia sobre la intencion en la application de la Santa Misa, VII-104 pp., 1931.

63. Frey, Rev. Wolfgang Norbert, O.S.B., A.B., J.C.D., The Act of Religious Profession, VIII-174 pp., 1931.
64. Roberts, Rev. James Brendan, A.B., J.C.D., The Banns of Marriage, XIV-140 pp., 1931.
65. Ryder, Rev. Raymond Aloysius, A.B., J.C.D., Simony, IX-151 pp., 1931.
66. Campagna, Rev. Angelo, Ph.D., J.U.D., Il Vicario Generale del Vescovo, VII-205, pp., 1931.
67. Cox, Rev. Joseph Godfrey, A.B., J.C.D., The Administration of Seminaries, VI-124 pp., 1931.
68. Gregory, Rev. Donald J., J.U.D., The Pauline Privilege, XV-165 pp., 1931.
69. Donohue, Rev. John F., J.C.D., The Impediment of Crime, VII-110 pp., 1931.
70. Dooley, Rev. Eugene A., O.M.I., J.C.D., Church Law on Sacred Relics, IX-143 pp., 1931.
71. Orth, Rev. Clement Raymond, O.M.C., J.C.D., The Approbation of Religious Institutes, 171 pp., 1931.
72. Pernicone, Rev. Joseph M., A.B., J.C.D., The Ecclesiastical Prohibition of Books, XII-267 pp., 1932.
73. Clinton, Rev. Connell, A.B., J.C.D., The Paschal Precept, IX-108 pp., 1932.
74. Donnelly, Rev. Francis B., A.M., S.T.L., J.C.D., The Diocesan Synod, VIII-125 pp., 1932.
75. Torrente, Rev. Camilo, C.M.F., J.C.D., Las Procesiones Sagradas, V-145 pp., 1932.
76. Murphy, Rev. Edwin J., C.PP.S., J.C.D., Suspension Ex Informata Conscientia, XI-122 pp., 1932.
77. MacKenzie, Rev. Eric F., A.M., S.T.L., J.C.D., The Delict of Heresy in its Commission, Penalization, Absolution, VII-124 pp., 1932.
78. Lyons, Rev. Avitus E., S.T.B., J.C.D., The Collegiate Tribunal of First Instance, XI-147 pp., 1932.
79. Connolly, Rev. Thomas A., J.C.D., Appeals, XI-195 pp., 1932.
80. Sangmeister, Rev. Joseph V., A.B., J.C.D., Force and Fear as Precluding Matrimonial Consent, V-211 pp., 1932.
81. Jaeger, Rev. Leo A., A.B., J.C.D., The Administration of Vacant and Quasi-Vacant Episcopal Sees in the United States, IX-229 pp., 1932.
82. Rimlinger, Rev. Herbert T., J.C.D., Error Invalidating Matrimonial Consent, VII-79 pp., 1932.
83. Barrett, Rev. John D. M., S.S., J.C.D., A Comparative Study of the Councils of Baltimore and the Code of Canon Law, IX-223 pp., 1932.
84. Carberry, Rev. John J., Ph.D., S.T.D., J.C.D., The Juridical Form of Marriage, X-177 pp., 1934.
85. Dolan, Rev. John L., A.B., J.C.D., The Defensor Vinculi, XII-157 pp., 1934.

86. Hannan, Rev. Jerome D., A.M., S.T.D., LL.B., J.C.D., The Canon Law of Wills, IX-517 pp., 1934.
87. Lemieux, Rev. Delise A., A.M., J.C.D., The Sentence in Ecclesiastical Procedure, IX-131 pp., 1934.
88. O'Rourke, Rev. James J., A.B., J.C.D., Parish Registers, VII-109 pp., 1934.
89. Timlin, Rev. Bartholomew, O.F.M., A.M., J.C.D., Conditional Matrimonial Consent, X-381 pp., 1934.
90. Wahl, Rev. Francis X., A.B., J.C.D., The Matrimonial Impediments of Consanguinity and Affinity, VI-125 pp., 1934.
91. White, Rev. Robert J., A.B., LL.B., S.T.B., J.C.D., Canonical Ante-Nuptial Promises and the Civil Law, VI-152 pp., 1934.
92. Herrera, Rev. Antonio Parra, O.C.D., J.C.D., Legislacion Ecclesiastica sobra el Ayuno y la Abstinencia, XI-191 pp., 1935.
93. Kennedy, Rev. Edwin J., J.C.D., The Special Matrimonial Process in Cases of Evident Nullity, X-165 pp., 1935.
94. Manning, Rev. John J., A.B., J.C.D., Presumption of Law in Matrimonial Procedure, XI-111 pp., 1935.
95. Moeder, Rev. John M., J.C.D., The Proper Bishop for Ordination and Dismissorial Letters, VII-135 pp., 1935.
96. O'Mara, Rev. William A., A.B., J.C.D., Canonical Causes for Matrimonial Dispensations, IX-155 pp., 1935.
97. Reilly, Rev. Peter, J.C.D., Residence of Pastors, IX-81 pp., 1935.
98. Smith, Rev. Mariner T., O.P., S.T.Lr., J.C.D., The Penal Law for Religious, VIII-169 pp., 1935.
99. Whalen, Rev. Donald W., A.M., J.C.D., The Value of Testimonial Evidence in Matrimonial Procedure, XIII-297 pp., 1935.
100. Cleary, Rev. Joseph F., J.C.D., Canonical Limitations on the Alienation of Church Property, VIII-141 pp., 1936.
101. Glynn, Rev. John C., J.C.D., The Promoter of Justice, XX-337 pp., 1936.
102. Brennan, Rev. James H., S.S., M.A., S.T.B., J.C.D., The Simple Convalidation of Marriage, VI-135 pp., 1937.
103. Brunini, Rev. Joseph Bernard, J.C.D., The Clerical Obligations of Canons 139 and 142, X-121 pp., 1937.
104. Connor, Rev. Maurice, A.B., J.C.D., The Administrative Removal of Pastors, VIII-159 pp., 1937.
105. Guilfoyle, Rev. Merlin Joseph, J.C.D., Custom, XI-144 pp., 1937.
106. Hughes, Rev. James Austin, A.B., A.M., J.C.D., Witnesses in Criminal Trials of Clerics, IX-140 pp., 1937.
107. Jansen, Rev. Raymond J., A.B., S.T.L., J.C.D., Canonical Provisions for Catechetical Instruction, VII-153 pp., 1937.
108. Kealy, Rev. John James, A.B., J.C.D., The Introductory Libellus in Church Court Procedure, XI-121 pp., 1937.

109. McManus, Rev. James Edward, C.SS.R., J.C.D., The Administration of Temporal Goods in Religious Institutes, XVI-196 pp., 1937.
110. Moriarty, Rev. Eugene James, J.C.D., Oaths in Ecclesiastical Courts, X-115 pp., 1937.
111. Rainer, Rev. Eligius George, C.SS.R., J.C.D., Suspension of Clerics, XVII-249 pp., 1937.
112. Reilly, Rev. Thomas F., C.SS.R., J.C.D., Visitation of Religious, VI-195 pp., 1938.
113. Moriarty, Rev. Francis E., C.SS.R., J.C.D., The Extraordinary Absolution from Censures, XV-334 pp., 1938.
114. Connolly, Rev. Nicholas P., J.C.D., The Canonical Erection of Parishes, X-132 pp., 1938.
115. Donovan, Rev. James Joseph, J.C.D., The Pastor's Obligation in Prenuptial Investigation, XII-322 pp., 1938.
116. Harrigan, Rev. Robert J., M.A., S.T.B., J.C.D., The Radical Sanation of Invalid Marriages, VIII-208 pp., 1938.
117. Boffa, Rev. Conrad Humbert, J.C.D., Canonical Provisions for Catholic Schools, VII-211 pp., 1939.
118. Parsons, Rev. Anscar John, O.M.Cap., J.C.D., Canonical Elections, XII-236 pp., 1939.
119. Reilly, Rev. Edward Michael, A.B., J.C.D., The General Norms of Dispensation, XII-156 pp., 1939.
120. Ryan, Rev. Gerald Aloysius, A.B., J.C.D., Principles of Episcopal Jurisdiction, XII-172 pp., 1939.
121. Burton, Rev. Francis James, C.S.C., A.B., J.C.D., A Commentary on Canon 1125, X-222 pp., 1940.
122. Miaskiewicz, Rev. Francis Sigismund, J.C.D., Supplied Jurisdiction According to Canon 209, XII-340 pp., 1940.
123. Rice, Rev. Patrick William, A.B., J.C.D., Proof of Death in Prenuptial Investigation, VIII-156 pp., 1940.
124. Anglin, Rev. Thomas Francis, M.S., J.C.D., The Eucharistic Fast, VIII-183 pp., 1941.
125. Coleman, Rev. John Jerome, J.C.D., The Minister of Confirmation, VI-153 pp., 1941.
126. Downs, Rev. John Emmanuel, A.B., J.C.D., The Concept of Clerical Immunity, XI-163 pp., 1941.
127. Esswein, Rev. Anthony Albert, J.C.D., Extrajudicial Penal Powers of Ecclesiastical Superiors, X-144 pp., 1941.
128. Farrell, Rev. Benjamin Francis, M.A., S.T.L., J.C.D., The Rights and Duties of the Local Ordinary Regarding Congregations of Women Religious of Pontifical Approval, V-195 pp., 1941.
129. Feeney, Rev. Thomas John, A.B., S.T.L., J.C.D., Restitutio in Integrum, VI-169 pp., 1941.
130. Findlay, Rev. Stephen William, O.S.B., A.B., J.C.D., Canonical Norms Governing the Deposition and Degradation of Clerics, XVII-279 pp., 1941.

131. Goodwine, Rev. John, A.B., S.T.L., J.C.D., The Right of the Church to Acquire Property, VIII-119 pp., 1941.
132. Heston, Rev. Edward Louis, C.S.C., Ph.D., S.T.D., J.C.D., The Alienation of Church Property in the United States, XII-222 pp., 1941.
133. Hogan, Rev. James John, A.B., S.T.L., J.C.D., Judicial Advocates and Procurators, XIII-200 pp., 1941.
134. Kealy, Rev. Thomas M., A.B., Litt.B., J.C.D., Dowry of Women Religious, IX-152 pp., 1941.
135. Keene, Rev. Michael James, O.S.B., J.C.D., Religious Ordinaries and Canon 198, V-164 pp., 1941 (printed 1942).
136. Kerin, Rev. Charles A., S.S., M.A., S.T.B., J.C.D., The Privation of Christian Burial, XVI-279 pp., 1941.
137. Louis, Rev. William Francis, M.A., J.C.D., Diocesan Archives, X-101 pp., 1941.
138. McDevitt, Rev. Gilbert Joseph, A.B., J.C.D., Legitimacy and Legitimation, X-247 pp., 1941.
139. McDonough, Rev. Thomas Joseph, A.B., J.C.D., Apostolic Administrators, X-217 pp., 1941.
140. Meier, Rev. Carl Anthony, A.B., J.C.D., Penal Administrative Procedure Against Negligent Pastors, XI-240 pp., 1941.
141. Schmidt, Rev. John Rogg, A.B., J.C.D., The Principles of Authentic Interpretation in Canon 17 of the Code of Canon Law, XII-331 pp., 1941.
142. Slafkosky, Rev. Andrew Leonard, A.B., J.C.D., The Canonical Episcopal Visitation of the Diocese, X-197 pp., 1941.
143. Swoboda, Rev. Innocent Robert, O.F.M., J.C.D., Ignorance in Relation to the Imputability of Delicts, IX-271 pp., 1941.
144. Dubé, Rev. Arthur Joseph, A.B., J.C.D., The General Principles for the Reckoning of Time in Canon Law, VIII-299 pp., 1941.
145. McBride, Rev. James T., A.B., J.C.D., Incardination and Excardination of Seculars, XX-585 pp., 1941.
146. Król, Rev. John T., J.C.D., The Defendant in Ecclesiastical Trials, XII-207 pp., 1942.
147. Comyns, Rev. Joseph J., C.SS.R., A.B., J.C.D., Papal and Episcopal Administration of Church Property, XIV-155 pp., 1942.
148. Barry, Rev. Garrett Francis, O.M.I., J.C.D., Violation of the Cloister, XII-260 pp., 1942.
149. Bolduc, Rev. Gatien, C.S.V., A.B., S.T.L., J.C.D., Les Études dans les Religious Cléricales, VIII-155 pp., 1942.
150. Boyle, Rev. David John, M.A., J.C.D., The Juridic Effects of Moral Certitude on Pre-Nuptial Guarantees, XII-188 pp., 1942.
151. Canavan, Rev. Walter Joseph, M.A., Litt.D., J.C.D., The Profession of Faith, XII-143 pp., 1942.
152. Desrochers, Rev. Bruno, A.B., Ph.L., S.T.B., J.C.D., Le Premier Concile Plénier de Québec et le Code de Droit Canonique, XIV-186 pp., 1942.

153. DILLON, REV. ROBERT EDWARD, A.B., J.C.D., Common Law Marriage, X-148 pp., 1942.
154. DODWELL, REV. EDWARD JOHN, PH.D., S.T.B., J.C.D., The Time and Place for the Celebration of Marriage, X-156 pp., 1942.
155. DONNELLAN, REV. THOMAS ANDREW, A.B., J.C.D., The Obligation of the Missa pro Populo, VII-131 pp., 1942.
156. ELTZ, REV. LOUIS ANTHONY, A.B., J.C.D., Cooperation in Crime, XII-208 pp., 1942.
157. GASS, REV. SYLVESTER FRANCIS, M.A., J.C.D., Ecclesiastical Pensions, XI-206 pp., 1942.
158. GUINIVEN, REV. JOHN JOSEPH, C.SS.R., J.C.D., The Precept of Hearing Mass, XIV-188 pp., 1942.
159. GULCZYNSKI, REV. JOHN THEOPHILUS, J.C.D., The Desecration and Violation of Churches, X-126 pp., 1942.
160. HAMMILL, REV. JOHN LEO, M.A., J.C.D., The Obligations of the Traveler According to Canon 14, VIII-204 pp., 1942.
161. HAYDT, REV. JOHN JOSEPH, A.B., J.C.D., Reserved Benefices, XI-148 pp., 1942.
162. HUSER, REV. ROGER JOHN, O.F.M., A.B., J.C.D., The Crime of Abortion in Canon Law, XII-187 pp., 1942.
163. KEARNEY, REV. FRANCIS PATRICK, A.B., S.T.L., J.C.D., The Principles of Canon Law 1127, X-162 pp., 1942.
164. LINAHEN, REV. LEO JAMES, S.T.L., J.C.D., De Absolutione Complicis in Peccato Turpi, V-114 pp., 1942.
165. MCCLOSKEY, REV. JOSEPH ALOYSIUS, A.B., J.C.D., The Subject of Ecclesiastical Law According to Canon 12, XVII-246 pp., 1942 (printed 1943).
166. O'NEILL, REV. FRANCIS JOSEPH, C.SS.R., J.C.D., The Dismissal of Religious in Temporary Vows, XIII-220 pp., 1942.
167. PRINCE, REV. JOHN EDWARD, A.B., S.T.B., J.C.D., The Diocesan Chancellor, X-136 pp., 1942.
168. RIESNER, REV. ALBERT JOSEPH, C.SS.R., J.C.D., Apostates and Fugitives from Religious Institutes, IX-168 pp., 1942.
169. STENGER, REV. JOSEPH BERNARD, J.C.D., The Mortgaging of Church Property, 186 pp., 1942.
170. WALDRON, REV. JOSEPH FRANCIS, A.B., J.C.D., The Minister of Baptism, XII-197 pp., 1942.
171. WILLETT, REV. ROBERT ALBERT, J.C.D., The Probative Value of Documents in Ecclesiastical Trials, X-124 pp., 1942.
172. WOEBER, REV. EDWARD MARTIN, M.A., J.C.D., The Interpellations, XII-161 pp., 1942.
173. BENKO, REV. MATTHEW ALOYSIUS, O.S.B., M.A., J.C.D., The Abbot *Nullius*, XVI-148 pp., 1943.
174. CHRIST, REV. JOSEPH JAMES, M.A., S.T.L., J.C.D., Dispensation from Vindicative Penalties, XIV-285 pp., 1943.
175. CLANCY, REV. PATRICK M. J., O.P., A.B., S.T.Lr., J.C.D., The Local Religious Superior, X-229 pp., 1943.

176. Clarke, Rev. Thomas James, J.C.D., Parish Societies, XII-147 pp., 1943.
177. Connolly, Rev. John Patrick, S.T.L., J.C.D., Synodical Examiners and Parish Priest Consultors, X-223 pp., 1943.
178. Drumm, Rev. William Martin, A.B., J.C.D., Hospital Chaplains, XII-175 pp., 1943.
179. Flanagan, Rev. Bernard Joseph, A.B., S.T.L., J.C.D., The Canonical Erection of Religious Houses, X-147 pp., 1943.
180. Kelleher, Rev. Stephen Joseph, A.B., S.T.B., J.C.D., Discussions with Non-Catholics: Canonical Legislation, X-93 pp., 1943.
181. Lewis, Rev. Gordian, C.P., J.C.D., Chapters in Religious Institutes, XII-169 pp., 1943.
182. Marx, Rev. Adolph, J.C.D., The Declaration of Nullity of Marriages Contracted Outside the Church, X-151 pp., 1943.
183. Matulenas, Rev. Raymond Anthony, O.S.B., A.B., J.C.D., Communication, a Source of Privileges, VII-225 pp., 1943.
184. O'Leary, Rev. Charles Gerard, C.SS.R., J.C.D., Religious Dismissed After Perpetual Profession, X-213 pp., 1943.
185. Power, Rev. Cornelius Michael, J.C.D., The Blessing of Cemeteries, XII-231 pp., 1943.
186. Shuhler, Rev. Ralph Vincent, O.S.A., J.C.D., Privileges of Religious to Absolve and Dispense, XII-195 pp., 1943.
187. Ziolkowski, Rev. Thaddeus Stanislaus, A.B., J.C.D., The Consecration and Blessing of Churches, XII-151 pp., 1943.
188. Heneghan, Rev. John Joseph, S.T.D., J.C.D., The Marriages of Unworthy Catholics: Canons 1065 and 1066, XVI-213 pp., 1944.
189. Carroll, Rev. Coleman Francis, M.A., S.T.L., J.C.L., Charitable Institutions.
190. Ciesluk, Rev. Joseph Edward, Ph.B., S.T.L., J.C.D., National Parishes in the United States, VI-178 pp., 1944.
191. Coburn, Rev. Vincent Paul, A.B., J.C.D., Marriages of Conscience, XII-172 pp., 1944.
192. Connors, Rev. Charles Paul, C.S.Sp., A.B., J.C.D., Extra-Judicial Procurators in the Code of Canon Law, X-94 pp., 1944.
193. Coyle, Rev. Paul Raymond, A.B., J.C.D., Judicial Exceptions, X-142 pp., 1944.
194. Fair, Rev. Bartholomew Francis, A.B., S.T.L., J.C.D., The Impediment of Abduction, XII-122 pp., 1944.
195. Gallagher, Rev. Thomas Raphael, O.P., A.B., S.T.Lr., J.C.D., The Examination of the Qualities of the Ordinand, X-166 pp., 1944.
196. Gannon, Rev. John Mark, S.T.L., J.C.D., The Interstices Required for the Promotion to Orders, XII-100 pp., 1944.
197. Goldsmith, Rev. J. William, B.C.S., S.T.L., J.C.D., The Competence of Church and State Over Marriages—Disputed Points, X-128 pp., 1944.

198. GOODWINE, REV. JOSEPH GERARD, A.B., S.T.B., J.C.D., The Reception of Converts, XIV-326 pp., 1944.
199. KOWALSKI, REV. ROMUALD EUGENE, O.F.M., A.B., J.C.D., Sustenance of Religious Houses of Regulars, X-174 pp., 1944.
200. McCOY, REV. ALAN EDWARD, O.F.M., J.C.D., Force and Fear in Relation to Delictual Imputability and Penal Responsibility, XII-160 pp., 1944.
201. McDEVITT, REV. VINCENT JOHN, PH.B., S.T.L., J.C.L., Perjury.
202. MARTIN, REV. THOMAS OWEN, PH.D., S.T.D., J.C.D., Adverse Possession, Prescription and Limitation of Actions: The Canonical "Praescriptio," XX-208 pp., 1944.
203. MIKLOSOVIC, REV. PAUL JOHN, A.B., J.C.L., Attempted Marriages and Their Consequent Juridic Effects.
204. MUNDY, REV. THOMAS MAURICE, A.B., S.T.L., J.C.D., The Union of Parishes, X-164 pp. 1944.
205. O'DEA, REV. JOHN COYLE, A.B., J.C.D., The Matrimonial Impediment of Nonage, VIII-126 pp., 1944.
206. OLALIA, REV. ALEXANDER AYSON, S.T.L., J.C.D., A Comparative Study of the Christian Constitution of States and the Constitution of the Philippine Commonwealth, XII-136 pp., 1944.
207. POISSON, REV. PIERRE-MARIE, C.S.C., A.B., PH.L., TH.L., J.C.L., Droits Patrimoniaux des Maisons et des Eglises Religieuses.
208. STADALNIKAS, REV. CASIMIR JOSEPH, M.I.C., J.C.D., Reservation of Censures, X-141 pp., 1944.
209. SULLIVAN, REV. EUGENE HENRY, S.T.L., J.C.D., Proof of the Reception of the Sacraments, X-165 pp., 1944.
210. VAUGHAN, REV. WILLIAM EDWARD, J.C.D., Constitutions for Diocesan Courts, X-200 pp., 1944.
211. PARO, REV. GINO, S.T.D., J.C.D., The Right of Papal Legation, X-221 pp., 1944 (printed 1947).
212. BALZER, REV. RALPH FRANCIS, C.P., J.C.D., The Computation of Time in a Canonical Novitiate, X-227 pp., 1945.
213. DOUGHERTY, REV. JOHN WHELAN, A.B., S.T.L., J.C.D., De Inquisitione Speciali, XII-195 pp., 1945.
214. DZIOB, REV. MICHAEL WALTER, J.C.D., The Sacred Congregation for the Oriental Church, XII-181 pp., 1945.
215. EIDENSCHINK, REV. JOHN ALBERT, O.S.B., B.A., J.C.D., The Election of Bishops in the Letters of Pope Gregory the Great, VIII-200 pp., 1945.
216. GILL, REV. NICHOLAS, C.P., J.C.D., The Spiritual Prefect in Clerical Religious Houses of Study, X-140 pp., 1945.
217. HYNES, REV. HARRY GERARD, S.T.L., J.C.D., The Privileges of Cardinals, XII-183 pp., 1945.
218. McDEVITT, REV. GERALD VINCENT, S.T.L., J.C.D., The Renunciation of an Ecclesiastical Office, XIV-179 pp., 1945.

219. MANNING, REV. JOSEPH LEROY, J.C.D., The Free Conferral of Offices, VII-116 pp., 1945.
220. MEYER, REV. LOUIS G., O.S.B., A.B., S.T.B., J.C.D., Alms-gathering by Religious, XII-163 pp., 1945.
221. O'DONNELL, REV. CLETUS FRANCIS, M.A., J.C.D., The Marriage of Minors, XII-268 pp., 1945.
222. PRUNSKIS, REV. JOSEPH, J.C.D., Comparative Law, Ecclesiastical and Civil, in Lithuanian Concordat, X-161 pp., 1945.
223. SWEENEY, REV. FRANCIS PATRICK, C.SS.R., J.C.D., The Reduction of Clerics to the Lay State, X-199 pp., 1945.
224. VOGELPOHL, REV. HENRY JOHN, J.C.D., The Simple Impediments to Holy Orders, XVI-190 pp., 1945.
225. BROCKHAUS, REV. THOMAS AQUINAS, O.S.B., J.C.D., Religious who are known as *Conversi*, X-127 pp., 1945.
226. GRIESE, REV. ORVILLE NICHOLAS, S.T.D., J.C.D., The Marriage Contract and the Procreation of Offspring, XVI-224 pp., 1946.
227. BOUDREAUX, REV. WARREN LOUIS, J.C.D., The *"ab acatholicis nati"* of Canon 1099, § 2, XII-110 pp., 1946.
228. BOWE, REV. THOMAS JOSEPH, A.B., J.C.D., Religious Superioresses, VIII-206 pp., 1946.
229. DIEDERICHS, REV. MICHAEL FERDINAND, S.C.J., J.C.D., The Jurisdiction of the Latin Ordinaries over their Oriental Subjects, XIV-153 pp., 1946.
230. DINGMAN, REV. MAURICE JOHN, A.B., S.T.L., J.C.L., The Plaintiff in Contentious Trials.
231. FRISON, REV. BASIL, C.M.F., M.MUS., J.C.D., The Retroactivity of Law, X-221 pp., 1946.
232. CALVIN, REV. WILLIAM ANTHONY, M.A., J.C.D., The Administrative Transfer of Pastors, XII-288 pp., 1946.
233. GORACY, REV. JOSEPH C., J.C.L., The Diriment Matrimonial Impediment of Major Orders.
234. HALE, REV. JOSEPH FRANCIS, M.A., S.T.L., J.C.D., The Pastor of Burial, X-247 pp., 1946 (printed 1949).
235. HENRY, REV. JOSEPH ARTHUR, A.B., J.C.D., The Mass and Holy Communion: Interritual Law, XII-138 pp., 1946.
236. LINENBERGER, REV. HERBERT, C.PP.S., J.C.D., The False Denunciation of an Innocent Confessor, VIII-205 pp., 1946 (1949).
237. LOWRY, REV. JAMES MARTIN, A.B., J.C.D., Dispensation from Private Vows, XII-266 pp., 1946.
238. LYNCH, REV. GEORGE EDWARD, A.B., S.T.L., J.C.D., Coadjutors and Auxiliaries of Bishops, X-107 pp., 1946 (printed 1947).
239. LYNCH, REV. TIMOTHY, M.S.SS.T., J.C.D., Contracts between Bishops and Religious Congregations, XIII-232 pp., 1946.
240. McCLUNN, REV. JUSTIN DAVID, A.B., S.T.L., J.C.D., Administrative Recourse, VII-142 pp., 1946.

241. LOHMULLER, REV. MARTIN NICHOLAS, A.B., J.C.D., The Promulgation of Law, XII-140 pp., 1947.
242. MCGRATH, REV. JAMES, A.B., J.C.D., The Privilege of the Canon, XII-156 pp., 1946.
243. MARBACH, REV. JOSEPH FRANCIS, A.B., J.C.D., Marriage Legislation for the Catholics of the Oriental Rites in the United States and Canada, XIV-314 pp., 1946.
244. SHIMKUS, REV. BERNARD ALOYSIUS, A.B., J.C.L., The Determination and Transfer of Rite.
245. SMITH, REV. VINCENT MICHAEL, A.B., S.T.L., J.C.L., Ignorance Affecting Matrimonial Consent.
246. WACHTRLE, REV. PAUL ANTHONY, A.B., J.C.L., The Baptism of the Children of Non-Catholics.
247. CROTTY, REV. MATTHEW MICHAEL, J.C.D., The Recipient of First Holy Communion, X-142 pp., 1947.
248. EAGLETON, REV. GEORGE, J.C.D., The Quinquennial Faculties, Formula IV, XIV-199 pp., 1947 (printed 1948).
249. GIBBONS, REV. MARION LEO, C.M., J.C.L., Domicile of the Wife Unlawfully Separated from Her Husband, XIV-171 pp., 1947.
250. KELLY, REV. BERNARD M., S.T.L., J.C.D., The Functions Reserved to Pastors, XII-141 pp., 1947.
251. KILCULLEN, REV. THOMAS J., LL.M., J.C.D., The Collegiate Moral Person as Party Litigant, X-150 pp., 1947.
252. LAFONTAINE, REV. GERMAINE JOSEPH, W.F., J.C.D., Relations Canoniques entre le Missionaire et Ses Superieurs, X-117 pp., 1947.
253. LANE, REV. LORAS THOMAS, A.B., S.T.L., J.C.D., Matrimonial Procedure in the Ordinary Court of Second Instance, XVI-184 pp., 1947.
254. LOVER, REV. JAMES FRANCIS, C.Ss.R., J.C.D., The Master of Novices, X-168 pp., 1947.
255. MCNICHOLAS, REV. TIMOTHY JOSEPH, J.C.D., The *Septimae Manus* Witness, XII-133 pp., 1947 (printed 1949).
256. MAROSITZ, REV. JOSEPH JOHN, M.S.C., J.C.D., Obligations and Privileges of Religious Promoted to the Episcopal or Cardinalitial Dignities, XII-180 pp., 1947.
257. MURPHY, REV. FRANCIS JOSEPH, J.C.D., Legislative Powers of the Provincial Council, XII-158 pp., 1947.
258. O'BRIEN, REV. ROMAEUS WILLIAM, O.CARM., J.C.D., The Provincial Superior in Religious Orders of Men, X-294 pp., 1947.
259. PFALLER, REV. BENEDICT ANTHONY, O.S.B., J.C.D., *The ipso facto* Effected Dismissal of Religious, XII-225 pp., 1947.
260. POPEK, REV. ALPHONSE SYLVESTER, J.C.D., The Rights and Obligations of Metropolitans, XX-460 pp., 1947.
261. RISTUCCIA, REV. BERNARD JOSEPH, C.M., J.C.D., Quasi-Religious, XVI-318 pp., 1947 (printed 1949).
262. SONNTAG, REV. NATHANIEL LOUIS, O.F.M.CAP., J.C.D., Censorship of Special Classes of Books, XII-147 pp., 1947.

263. STADLER, REV. JOSEPH NICHOLAS, J.C.D., Frequent Holy Communion, X-158 pp., 1947.
264. SZAL, REV. IGNATIUS JOSEPH, J.C.D., The Communication of Catholics with Schismatics, XII-217 pp., 1947.
265. WAGNER, REV. URBAN S., O.F.M., CONV., J.C.D., Parochial Substitute Vicars and Supplying Priests, IX-126 pp., 1947.
266. QUINN, REV. JOSEPH, M.A., J.C.D., Documents Required for the Reception of Orders, XIV-207 pp., 1948.
267. BENNINGTON, REV. JAMES CLEMENT, A.B., J.C.L., The Recipient of Confirmation.
268. BLAHER, REV. DAMIAN JOSEPH, O.F.M., A.B., J.C.D., The Ordinary Processes in Causes of Beatification and Canonization, XVI-290 pp., 1948 (printed 1949).
269. CLUNE, REV. ROBERT BELL, B.A., J.C.D., The Judicial Interrogation of the Parties, XII-142 pp., 1948.
270. COURTEMANCHE, REV. BASIL F., B.A., J.C.D., The Total Simulation of Matrimonial Consent, XX-120 pp., 1948.
271. DLOUHY, REV. MAUR JOHN, O.S.B., A.B., J.C.L., The Ordination of Exempt Religious.
272. DONOVAN, REV. JOHN THOMAS, PH.B., S.T.L., J.C.D., The Clerical Obligation of Canons 138 and 140, XII-209 pp., 1948.
273. FREKING, REV. FREDERICK W., A.B., S.T.B., J.C.D., The Canonical Installation of Pastors, XII-210 pp., 1948.
274. FULTON, REV. THOMAS B., J.C.D., Prenuptial Investigation, XII-190 pp., 1948.
275. GODLEY, REV. JAMES P., J.C.D., Time and Place for the Celebration of Mass, X-206 pp., 1948 (printed 1949).
276. KANE, REV. THOMAS A., A.B., B.S., J.C.D., Jurisdiction of the Patriarchs of the Major Sees in Antiquity and in the Middle Ages, XII-111 pp., 1948 (printed 1949).
277. KENNEDY, REV. ANDREW A., J.C.L., The Annual Pastoral Report to the Local Ordinary.
278. KONRAD, REV. JOSEPH GEORGE, J.C.D., Transfer of Religious to Another Community, VIII-284 pp., 1948 (printed 1949).
279. KRESS, REV. ALPHONSE, J.C.L., Contumacy in Ecclesiastical Trials.
280. MCCARTNEY, REV. MARCELLUS ANTHONY, O.F.M., M.A., J.C.D., Faculties of Regular Confessors, XII-164 pp., 1948 (printed 1949).
281. MCCASLIN, REV. EDWARD PATRICK, M.A., S.T.L., J.C.L., The Division of Parishes.
282. MCELROY, REV. FRANCIS J., A.B., J.C.L., The Privileges of Bishops.
283. QUINN, REV. STEPHEN, M.S.SS.T., J.C.D., Relation Between the Local Ordinary and Religious of Diocesan Approval, XII-153 pp., 1948 (printed 1949).
284. SCHNEIDER, REV. EDELHARD LOUIS, S.D.S., B.A., J.C.L., The Status of Secularized Ex-Religious Clerics, X-155 pp., 1948.

285. THOMPSON, CHESTER J., A.B., J.C.L., The Simple Removal from Office.
286. O'BRIEN, REV. KENNETH R., A.B., J.C.D., The Nature of Support of Diocesan Priests in the United States, XVI-162 pp., 1949.
287. METZ, REV. JOHN E., S.T.L., J.C.D., The Recording Judge in the Ecclesiastical Collegiate Tribunal, X-130 pp., 1949.
288. REINHARDT, REV. MARION J., S.T.L., J.C.D., The Rogatory Commission, XIII-182 pp., 1949.
289. ORTEGA UHIUK, REV. JUAN, S.J., J.C.L., De Delicto Sollicitationis.
290. CASEY, REV. JAMES V., J.C.D., A Study of Canon 2222 § 1, XII-127 pp., 1949.
291. ALLGEIER, REV. JOSEPH L., J.C.D., The Canonical Obligation of Preaching in Parish Churches, X-115 pp., 1949 (printed 1950).
292. CAHILL, REV. DANIEL R., J.C.D., The Custody of the Holy Eucharist, XVI-178 pp., 1949 (printed 1950).
293. CARR, REV. AIDEN, O.F.M., CARM., S.T.D., J.C.L., Vocation to the Priesthood: Its Canonical Concept.
294. KNOPKE, REV. ROCH F., O.F.M., J.C.D., Reverential Fear in Matrimonial Cases in Asiatic Countries: Rota Cases, XII-112 pp., 1949.
295. LAVELLE, REV. HOWARD D., J.C.D., The Obligation of Holding Sacred Missions in Parishes, XVI-142 pp., 1949.
296. MICKELLS, REV. ANTHONY B., J.C.L., The Constitutive Elements of Parishes.
297. NOONE, REV. JOHN J., J.C.D., Nullity in Judicial Acts, X-147 pp., 1949 (printed 1950).
298. SHEEHAN, REV. DANIEL E., J.C.L., The Minister of Holy Communion.
299. STATKUS, REV. FRANCIS J., J.C.L., The Minister of the Last Sacraments.
300. COOK, REV. JOHN P., J.C.D., Ecclesiastical Communities and Their Ability to Induce Legal Customs, XII-152 pp., 1949 (printed 1950).
301. FAZZALARO, REV. FRANCIS J., J.C.D., The Place for the Hearing of Confessions, X-150 pp., 1949 (printed 1950).
302. HANNAN, REV. PHILIP M., J.C.D., The Canonical Concept of *congrua sustentatio* for the Secular Clergy, XII-237 pp., 1949 (printed 1950).
303. QUINN, REV. HUGH G., S.T.L., J.C.L., The Particular Penal Precept.
304. GALLAGHER, REV. JOHN F., J.C.L., The Matrimonial Impediment of Public Propriety.
305. WELSH, REV. THOMAS J., J.C.L., The Use of the Portable Altar.
306. WATERS, REV. JOSEPH L., S.S.J., J.C.L., The Probation in Societies of Quasi-Religious.
307. REGAN, REV. MICHAEL J., J.C.L., Canon 16.
308. BYRNE, REV. HARRY J., J.C.L., Investment of Church Funds.
309. GALLAGHER, REV. THOMAS V., J.C.L., The Rejection of Judicial Witnesses and Testimony.
310. CHATHAM, REV. JOSIAH G., PH.B., S.T.L., J.C.L., Force and Fear as Invalidating Marriage: the Element of Injustice, XIV-183 pp., 1950.
311. BROWN, REV. JAMES VICTOR, O.R.S.A., J.C.L., The Invalidating Effects of Force, Fear, and Fraud Upon the Canonical Novitiate.

312. Duerr, Rev. Charles J., B.A., J.C.L., The Judicial Notary.
313. Gonzalez, Rev. Francisco J., O.S.A., J.C.L., De Parocho Religioso Eiusque Superiore Locali.
314. Hannon, Rev. James J., J.C.L., Holy Viaticum.
315. Sadlowski, Rev. Erwin L., J.C.L., The Sacred Furnishings of Churches.
316. Sego, Rev. Arthur A., J.C.L., Dispensation From the Interpellations.
317. Waterhouse, Rev. John M., J.C.L., The Power of the Local Ordinary to Impose a Matrimonial Ban.
318. Frein, Rev. Eugene B., J.C.L., The Discretionary Power of the Defender of the Matrimonial Bond.
319. Carton, Rev. George A., J.C.L., The Time Factor in the Gaining of Indulgences.
320. Walsh, Rev. John J., C.S.Sp., J.C.L., The Jurisdiction of the Interritual Confessor in the United States and Canada.
321. Unterkoefler, Rev. Ernest L., S.T.L., J.C.L., The Presiding Judge in Matrimonial Causes of First Instance.

www.ingramcontent.com/pod-product-compliance
Lightning Source LLC
LaVergne TN
LVHW050216080826
844660LV00012B/422

* 9 7 8 0 8 1 3 2 2 4 7 2 5 *